nation [ney-sh*uh*n] *noun* 1. An aggregation of persons of the same ethnic family, speaking the same language 2. A people of a particular territory, conscious of its unity to possess its own government

Canadian [kuh-ney-dee-uhn] *noun* 1. A native or inhabitant of Canada 2. Mike Myers

Mike Myers

Canada

Doubleday Canada

Doubleday Canada and colophon are registered trademarks of
Penguin Random House of Canada Limited.

Library and Archives Canada cataloguing in Publication
is available upon request.

ISBN: 978-0385-68925-0
e-book ISBN: 978-0385-68926-7

Book design by Terri Nimmo
Typeset by Erin Cooper
Printed and bound in the USA

Published in Canada by Doubleday Canada,
a division of Penguin Random House Canada Limited

www.penguinrandomhouse.ca

10 9 8 7 6 5 4 3 2 1

Penguin
Random House
DOUBLEDAY CANADA

I dedicate this book to my parents,
Eric and Bunny Myers.
Thanks for choosing Canada.

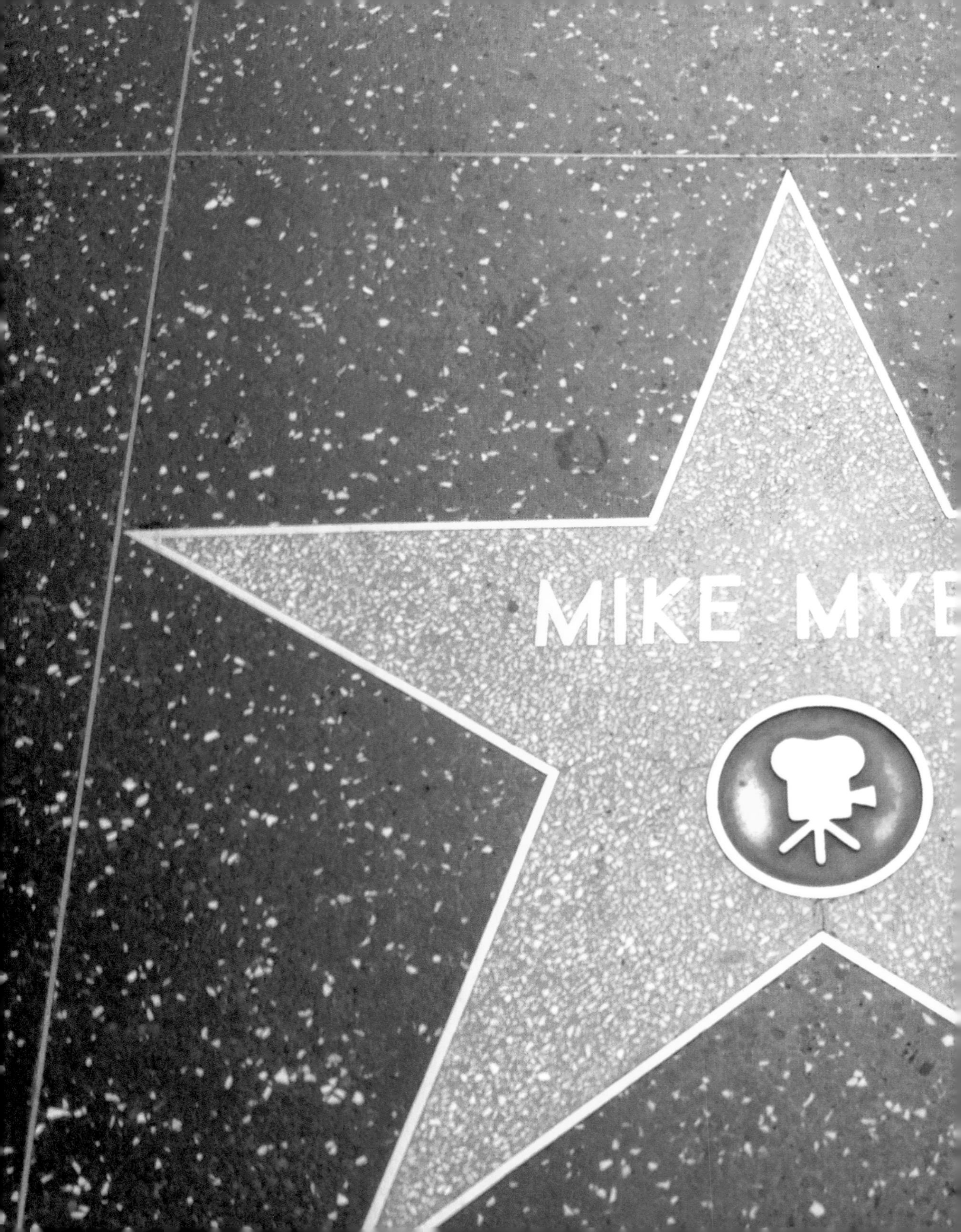
MIKE MYE

My Canada

I'M AN ACTOR, A WRITER, a producer, a director, a husband and a father, but no description of me is complete without saying that I'm a Canadian.

Legend has it that the late, great Canadian comedian John Candy was at Pearson Airport in Toronto one day when a baggage handler came up to him and said, "Wow, John Candy. Let me ask you something, John— why is it that when all you Canadian comedians make it big, you move down to the States?"

John Candy replied, "Actually, I live north of Toronto."

And the baggage handler said, "Aw, that's too bad. I thought you made it big, eh?"

That's what it is to be a famous Canadian, because Canadians aren't used to fame. Canada is not a famous country. The world knows nothing about us. Unlike America and Britain, our culture is not a culture for export.

John Candy was the first comedic actor in Hollywood history to be paid $1 million a movie. He was also known to be the most approachable person in the history of Hollywood. Supposedly, he was so approachable that in order to keep his films on schedule, the producers had to call him to the set half an hour earlier than they actually needed him, because he would stop and talk to every person that came up to him. He was genuinely interested in all who spoke to him because he didn't think he was better than anybody. He was a sweetheart.

In 1992, I had the great honour of meeting John Candy at Wayne Gretzky's restaurant, aptly named Wayne Gretzky's Toronto. I saw him from across the restaurant, but I was too starstruck to go over and say hello. He spotted me and came to my table (which blew my mind), and congratulated me on *Wayne's World,* which had just come out. He and Gretzky had just bought the Toronto Argonauts of the Canadian Football League. He was so generous of time, spirit, and encouragement. I had loved him as a performer, and now I loved him as a person. He was . . . Canadian: self-deprecating, unassuming, polite, considerate. He left this parting advice: "Never buy a sports team."

He was one of the greatest comedic actors ever, but he had no use for fame. Canadians are as capable of being starstruck as people from any other nation. But there is something in our character that distrusts fame. Marshall McLuhan, the famous Canadian intellectual who pioneered the field of media study, said of our homeland, "[Canadians are] the people who learned to live without the bold accents of the natural ego-trippers of other lands."

3

Drake. I'm so proud that he's Canadian. And I'm jealous of the brilliant way he gave T.O. a shout-out on his album cover by putting himself on the CN Tower. Well played, Drake, well played.

Right: Marshall McLuhan. This medium had a great message.

FAME IS A REAL EXPERIENCE, BUT IT'S NOT A CANADIAN EXPERIENCE, AND NOTHING ABOUT GROWING UP IN CANADA PREPARES YOU FOR A PUBLIC LIFE.

I've inherited the Canadian tendency of distrusting fame. Even though, ironically, I find myself, at the tender age of fifty-three, a public person. In this experience, I have learned that fame has no intrinsic value. I am grateful for it, of course, and I am much happier that it happened than I would be had it not happened. When I hear people complain about fame, it always sounds to me like, "Why do they pay me in gold bars? Gold bars are so heavy." But fame is not creativity, it's the industrial disease of creativity. Fame is a real experience, but it's not a Canadian experience, and nothing about growing up in Canada prepares you for a public life.

I only lived in Canada from 1963 until 1983, a mere twenty years. I have now lived outside of Canada for thirty-three years. I have indelible memories of my Canadian life, and since my departure I have been doing my best to keep track of my beloved country. My Canadian-ness affects every aspect of my being. My American friends once accused me of *enjoying* being Canadian. Guilty as charged.

Here's what is *not* going to be in this book: it is not going to be current with what's happening in Canada, especially in the arts. It's impossible to keep current about Canada when you live in the States, because even though we share the longest undefended border on earth, and we're each other's biggest trading partners, and NATO allies, and NORAD counterparts, you never hear any news about Canada when you live in the States.

At all.

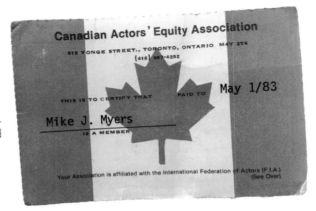

There was already a Mike Myers in Canadian Actors' Equity. I added the "J." as a nod to Michael J. Fox.

Ever.

Other things not in this book: any reference to the Meech Lake Accord. I'm not going to mention the Group of Seven painters, though I love them very much. There is nothing about the seal hunt (or seal harvest—tomato, tomahto). It will not contain a detailed account of Canada's shameful treatment of its Native people and the ongoing, complicated struggle to define and demark the relationship therein. I will right now, however, mention that, as progressive as Canada is, we are the only country to have actually completed a genocide against an indigenous people. The Beothuk were the indigenous people of Newfoundland. There is not one person left in the world who is fully Beothuk. They are all gone, forever. Shame. I'll let other books deal with this serious topic.

More pointedly, this is not a definitive history of Canada, nor is it a comprehensive portrait, or even strictly a memoir.

This book is about my fifty-three-year relationship with Canada, one that, for me, continues to grow and deepen. We may not live in the same house, but I think about Canada every day, and my American friends

The Confederation
Train is here

wonder why I just don't marry it already. I can't. I looked into it.

Some will read this book and say, "Why didn't you include this and why didn't you include that?" And my only response to those who feel that this book is missing something is to encourage them to write their own book, share their own story, which I would love to read.

As much as I love talking about my relationship with Canada, I'm always fascinated to hear what's going on for other Canadians. It's a unique experience to grow up in Canada, and when I explain it to non-Canadians, I feel like I am describing a dream I had, because the Canadian experience is not well known outside of Canada. But in describing this dream, I can tell you it's the opposite of a nightmare—it's a happy dream.

In 1967, Canada turned 100 years old. People all around the country made Centennial projects to honour this milestone. This book is my Centennial project, which I'm handing in a little late . . . sorry. But it will be on time for the Canadian Sesquicentennial. In 2017, Canada will turn 150. Happy birthday, Canada. Even after all these years, I still love you.

CANADA 150

PART ONE

True

CHAPTER ONE

Who Are We?
Why Are We?

THE GREAT CANADIAN
literary theorist Northrop Frye said that while most
countries' literature asks the question "Who am I?,"
Canadian literature asks the question "Where am I?"
Canada is an anomaly of both geography and history.
Canada is neither America, nor Great Britain, nor
France. There was never a mandate for Canada to
exist; it has existed by default. Canada is a country
born without a mission statement.

This lack of mission statement has created a crisis
of identity, which has created a crisis of confidence.
The most salient question is not "Where am I?" or
"Who am I?" but "Why am I?" And I think "Why am
I?" is at the heart of Canada's inner torment. Because
we don't know why we came to be, we have a low

11

self-image that puts us in a constant state of apology. We are in a sorry ("sore-y") state. Don't get me wrong, I love that Canada is polite, but we've taken apology to a burlesque level.

If a Mexican standoff is two people locked in an armed conflict for which there is seemingly no peaceful resolution, a Canadian standoff is when two Canadians come to a doorway, each of them beckoning the other to go first. Two Canadians will stand there for hours, because they'll say to themselves, "Who am I to go first?" When civility is taken too far, as it often is in the case of Canada, the entire country ends up stuck on the threshold, both literally and figuratively. We need to cross that threshold. Until we do, we won't have realized our full potential.

Culturally, the totem and taboo of Canada are not as clear as those of ancient, stifling, folkloric Europe. How straightforward and evident it is to be European. Could we expect Canada to compete with European cultures that have existed for centuries? Their history is literally carved into their cities. Toronto will often claim it's a world-class city. Paris simply claims it is Paris.

Let me illustrate. In Canada, if somebody came up and punched you, a Canadian would ask, "What did I do?" In America, if somebody randomly punched you, most Americans would ask, "What's that guy's problem?" America has more of a sense of itself than we do. They have a clear mission statement, we don't.

Americans individuated from stuffy old Europe by becoming the best storytellers in the world. They wrote their own powerful creation myth; they wrote their own powerful mission statement. It's been said that Rome ruled the world with the broadsword and the phalanx,

Opposite: This is my copy of the first issue, from 1975. Americans don't believe that there's a Captain Canuck, and they're even more surprised when I tell them Canadians invented Superman.

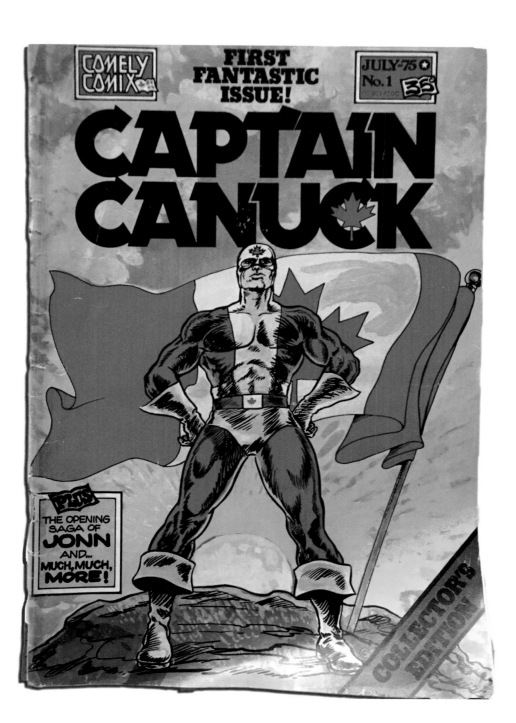

and Britain ruled the world with the three-masted ship. America, it seems, is ruling the world with the moving image. Hollywood industrialized mythology, and then weaponized it. It is widely believed that the Soviet Union folded because they couldn't compete with America's missile shield program, nicknamed Star Wars. I'd argue that the Soviets folded because they couldn't compete with the movie *Star Wars*. The Soviets must have seen the sheer mastery of American storytelling through *Star Wars* and thought, *Holy jumpin', they even have enough story power left over to create an entire immaculate universe? The story of dialectical materialism doesn't stand a chance.*

This is a birthday card my mum sent me. However, I think the artist may have taken a picture of me by Lake Ontario when I was a kid. I had that jacket. And notice— see page 56—that the Adidas has *four* stripes.

Americans have such a surplus of narrative that they've even created some of Canada's legend and lore. Take the Royal Canadian Mounted Police: it's known around the world that the Mounties "always get their man." In reality, the RCMP has a capture rate in line with most federal police forces. But this idea that "the Mounties always get their man" was created out of whole cloth in Hollywood.

It should be noted that too much mythmaking has a downside. For example, America is number 1 in confidence, but number 29 in education (Canada is number 10).

When Canada tries to create its own legend and lore, it falls short. For example, the city of Toronto had a contest to name the city's garbage cans. Torontonians sent in names like Gary Garbage, Tommy Trash, and Billy Bin.

Alas, the genius that is Ricky Receptacle.

The winner was Ricky Receptacle. I'll say it again: Ricky Receptacle.

While it's true that Canada lacks a mission statement, and this has been a source of national anxiety, I maintain that we actually know ourselves better than we think.

What we do know is that we're a country with the two solitudes of English Canada and French Canada. We do know that we are not so much a melting pot as we are a salad bowl. Up until recently, we had a Ministry of Multiculturalism. While we don't have a uniquely Canadian instrument, like America, which gave the world the banjo, the Ministry of Multiculturalism fostered respect for the indigenous instruments of each immigrant's home country. Canadians are also aware of the fact that we don't have a famous cuisine. In New York City, I'll go out for Italian, Chinese, or Mexican, but when's the last time you went out for Canadian? You didn't. And don't say poutine. That's a topping.

We know we don't have a "famous" cuisine, but we also know we do have "famous" ingredients. B.C. apples, Saskatchewan wheat, Nova Scotia salmon, and Manitoba . . . stuff. Ingredients are what help define Canada. Likewise, Canadian culture as a whole may not be famous, but the "ingredients" of our culture are. For example, we didn't invent folk music, but Saskatchewan's own Joni Mitchell perfected it. We

didn't invent rock and roll, but Ontario's own Neil Young redefined it, adding the "high lonesome" wail of the Canadian heartscape. America's Sweetheart, Mary Pickford, was born in Toronto. Canadian Mort Sahl, a contemporary of Lenny Bruce, is considered the father of American political satire. Andrew H. Malcolm said, "Canada was poised to have French culture, American efficiency, and British government. Instead, they got American culture, British efficiency, and French government."

In Canada in the 1960s, there was a contest to finish the following sentence: "As Canadian as . . . [blank]." Third place went to "As Canadian as hockey." Second place: "As Canadian as good government." Ultimately, the winner was, "As Canadian as possible under the circumstances." What are those circumstances? Well, one circumstance is our climate. In Canada, for eighteen days out of the year, if you don't have an artificial heat source, you'll die within forty-eight hours. Margaret Atwood and Northrop Frye said that this created, for Canadians, a "garrison mentality," whereby the central conflict of much of our literature is man versus nature. That sort of conflict breeds cooperation more than it breeds rugged individualism. It breeds caution more than it breeds entrepreneurialism. It's cold here. It's so cold it can make you cry. It's so cold you want your dad to come pick you up. Even when you're fifty-three years old.

In fact, winter is so part of the Canadian experience that there is a French Canadian folk song called "Mon

MARY PICKFORD

Born in 1893 in a house which stood near this site, Gladys Marie Smith appeared on stage in Toronto at the age of five. Her theatrical career took her to Broadway in 1907 where she adopted the name Mary Pickford. The actress's earliest film, "Her First Biscuits", was released by the Biograph Company in 1909 and she soon established herself as the international cinema's first great star. Her golden curls and children's roles endeared her to millions as "America's Sweetheart". She was instrumental in founding and directing a major film production company and starred in over fifty feature-length films including "Hearts Adrift", "Pollyanna" and "Coquette". For the last named film, she received the 1929 Academy Award as the year's best actress.

Erected by the Archeological and Historic Sites Board, Archives of Ontario

Pays." It goes, "*Mon pays, ce n'est pas un pays, c'est l'hiver*," or "My country is not a country, it's the winter." And in typical Canadian fashion, I only found out about this song when Patsy Gallant, a Canadian singer, co-opted the tune of "Mon Pays" but rewrote the lyrics to be about America, renaming "Mon Pays" to "From New York to L.A." It was a smash hit in the States. What little bit of Canadian culture we had was rewritten into American culture— as a disco song, no less.

We've spoken of geography and climate as elements that define us. Canadian history defines us as well, but tragically, it is boring. In fact, I have offered Canadian history lessons to my American insomniac friends. By the time I tell them about the Beaver Wars, my American friends are fast asleep. Canadian history could be a drug-free alternative to anaesthesia.

BY THE TIME I TELL THEM ABOUT THE BEAVER WARS, MY AMERICAN FRIENDS ARE FAST ASLEEP. CANADIAN HISTORY COULD BE A DRUG-FREE ALTERNATIVE TO ANAESTHESIA.

The problem with Canadian history mirrors the problem with the Canadian identity as a whole. Our history is a series of often-unconnected facts and events, not driven by a mission. There's no stated goal. In most movies, you know what the character wants by the end of Act One. Will he get the girl? Will he steal the gold? For the United States, the stated goal is, "Will the American Revolution survive?" We got nothing. Canada has had very few wars, and of those wars, none of them were protracted or bloody. Most national advancements came by way of legislation. We didn't have a gunfight at the O.K. Corral. America sent settlers west, who then formed police forces. Canada sent out the Mounties first, and then the settlers. Let's look at Canadian history . . . briefly.

In the 1500s, the French claimed the land the Iroquois called "Kanata" in the name of France.

In the 1600s, England established colonies in Newfoundland.

By the 1700s, Britain had defeated France in Canada (one conflict was called the Beaver Wars).

In 1776, America had a Revolution. Canada, however, remained loyal to the King.

In the War of 1812, Canada repelled an American invasion, ensuring Canadian independence from America. If you read a Canadian textbook, Canada won the War of 1812. If you read an American textbook, America won.

In 1867, Canada got its independence, not through an armed revolution, but through an unarmed evolution—a piece of British legislation called the British

Ah, the beaver. Our national animal, representing Canada's great outdoors, Canada's industriousness, and Canada's love of infantile jokes.

North America Act. Canada was the first country in the history of nation states to break peacefully from its mother country. More than anything, this shapes who we are.

Canada remained a Dominion of Britain, and would not get its own foreign policy until 1931, its own army until 1940, its own supreme court until 1949, and its own flag until 1965. Canada finally got its

Major-General Sir Isaac Brock. This British General repelled the American invasion at the Battle of Queenston Heights during the War of 1812. Even though he is English, he is one of my Canadian heroes. I did a project on him in Grade 6.

own constitution in 1982. That's how evolution rolls.

There is one bit of Canadian history that has always upset me. After World War II, Canada began to develop its own aviation industry. Its crowning achievement was the Avro CF-105 Arrow. The most advanced fighter jet in the world, designed by Canadians in Canada. In 1959, Conservative prime minister John Diefenbaker scrapped the Arrow in favour of the Bomarc missile system. He did this under pressure from the Americans, who, I'm sure, were not happy that Canada had stolen its lunch by designing such a cutting-edge piece of military hardware. It breaks my heart to think that we didn't realize our full potential. We didn't believe in ourselves, because we didn't have anything to believe in.

We do, however, believe in statistics.

Canadians are obsessed with statistics. Well, seven out of ten Canadians are obsessed with statistics. And of those seven, 25 percent of them . . . you get my point. Canadians love statistics so much that there is literally a branch of the government called Statistics Canada. Other cultures contemplate their own navel through literature and cinema. We keep lists. Ironically, one of the best books that lists Canadian achievements was written by an American, Ralph Nader. Included in Mr. Nader's list of Canadian achievements are items such as:

We invented time zones, the telephone, the first steamship, the zipper, the hydrofoil boat, the first short takeoff and landing plane, the first commercial jet transport, Pablum, the first credit union, socialized medicine, green ink, insulin, radiation therapy for cancer, the McIntosh apple, various strains of rust-resistant wheat, dry ginger ale, the chocolate bar, Greenpeace, IMAX film, the panoramic camera, the paint roller, the green garbage bag, lacrosse, basketball (we did!), synchronized swimming, the Blue Berets, Superman, the snowblower, the snowmobile, frozen food, ice hockey, virtually anything to do with the cold, and, of course, Trivial Pursuit.

We had the first publicly owned electric utility, the first plant to run on hydroelectricity, the first transatlantic cable, the first long-distance phone call, the first transatlantic wireless message, the first wireless voice message, the first radio voice broadcast, the first domestic geostationary satellite, the first steam foghorn, the first commercial motion picture, the first documentary, and the first motion picture showing in North America.

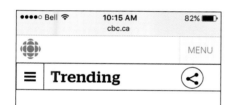

Canada's obsession with lists is not only a compensatory mechanism in the absence of identity, but it's also an effort to self-soothe. If you're French, you don't turn to someone and say, "Hi, I'm from France, home of Napoleon. We make wine, high-end cheese, and produce great artists like Chagall, Renoir, and Matisse." No, in fact, French people say, "Hi, I'm French." But, because nobody knows anything

HOBBY CRAFT
AVRO ARROW
CF-105
1/48 SCALE PLASTIC MODEL KIT
MODÈLE EN PLASTIQUE RÉDUIT À L'ÉCH
RL 201
25201

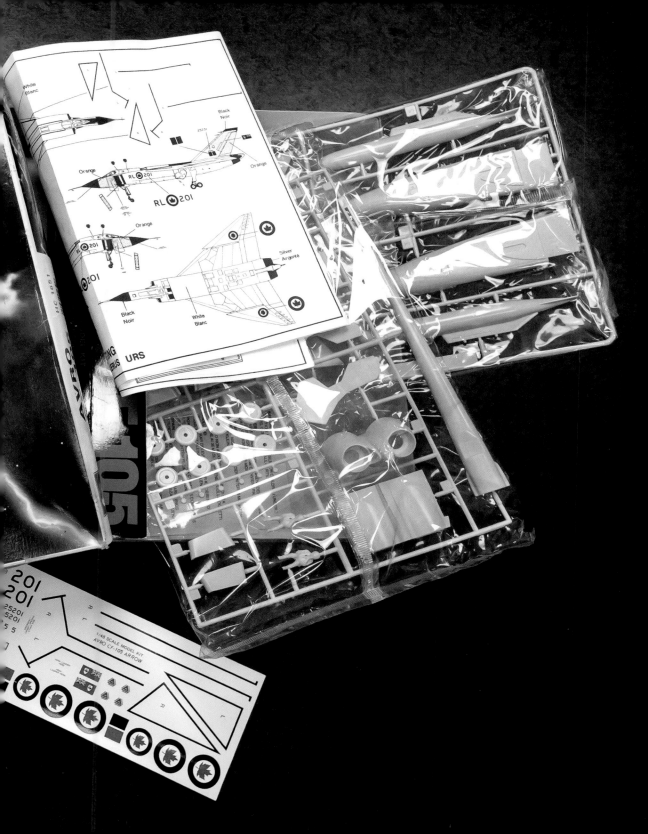

Above: Canada's own Wayne and Shuster. A staple of *The Ed Sullivan Show*. They planted the flag. So funny.

Right: Doug Henning, rock and roll illusionist. Martin Short's impression of him on *SCTV* is transcendent.

about Canada, we feel we have to produce a resumé after we say we're Canadian. It makes us feel good about ourselves.

Canadians love it when other countries mention Canada. I still get excited when I hear Carly Simon's 1972 song "You're So Vain," when she says, "Then you flew your Learjet up to Nova Scotia to see the total eclipse of the sun." My brothers and I would cheer when she mentioned Nova Scotia. I guess we thought this song was about us, didn't we, didn't we? But years before that, I remember being so proud when I saw Wayne and Shuster being introduced on *The Ed Sullivan Show* as "Canada's own Wayne and Shuster." Holy crap, Ed Sullivan just said "Canada." When Canadian Doug Henning, the long-haired illusionist who intro-duced rock music and rock costumes to the world of magic, mentioned that he was Canadian, we were thrilled. I also remember spotting an Ontario Provincial Police patch sewn on Paul McCartney's costume on the cover of *Sgt. Pepper*. Of course, at the time there was a rumour that Paul had died, and due to the fold on his jacket, the OPP patch appeared to read OPD, which, the conspiracy theorists argued, stood for "Officially Pronounced Dead." We knew it was the OPP. I can spot Canadiana in the parts per billion.

Then, too, of course, it was always great when Canadian artists who were popular in America would mention Canada. I get a little lump in my throat when Canada's Neil Young sings, in "Helpless," "There is

Opposite (bottom): From the *Sgt. Pepper's Lonely Hearts Club Band* cover. Note the Ontario Provincial Police patch. I can spot Canadiana in the parts per billion.

25

"If the central European experience is sex and the central mystery 'what goes on in the bedroom,' and the central American experience is killing and the central mystery is 'what goes on in the forest' (or in the slum streets), surely the central Canadian experience is death and the central mystery is 'what goes on in the coffin'."
MARGARET ATWOOD, *Survival.*

She is a Canadian genius. I hail you, Margaret Atwood.

a town in north Ontario." And when Joni sings in "A Case of You," "I drew a map of Canada, O Canada," I weep uncontrollably.

This sort of sentimentality is one of Canada's lesser-known traits. In fact, Canadians tend to be a bit . . . morbid. There, I said it: Canada is morbid. This morbidity is so subtle and so ingrained that I don't even think Canadians realize it. I didn't realize it myself until many years after I had left the country.

When Canadians tell you a story, they always insert morbid, often superfluous, details. For example:

MIKE: How's work?

CANADIAN: I got a promotion!

MIKE: Oh, that's great. Congratulations!

CANADIAN: Oh, thanks.
[*Pause, weird change of tone*]
You know my friend at work, Bill?

MIKE: Yeah?

CANADIAN: (*Gravely*)
He had a heart attack, eh?

MIKE: Oh, I'm so sorry. At work?

CANADIAN: (*Gravely, almost melodramatic*)
No, at home.
[*dramatic pause*]
In front of his kids, eh?

"In front of his kids, eh?" I can't tell you how many times Canadian stories end with "in front of his kids, eh?" It's as if Canadians don't have confidence that the information they're imparting to you is going to be interesting enough—that it needs a tragic element fused onto it, to get your attention. But this kind of morbid storytelling isn't confined to just local and personal events. Whenever a celebrity dies, I get texts.

And almost always, these texts are coming from a 416 area code (Toronto).

> Hey Mike, did you hear about Michael Jackson? He died. Sad, eh?

But this morbidity is drilled into us at an early age. At school every September, there would be an assembly welcoming the students back. Invariably, the assembly would include a list of teachers who had died over the summer. A disproportionate number of these teachers died either in horrific boating accidents or tragic hayrides somewhere "up north." Each of their deaths was described in uncomfortably graphic detail. It was almost like a police report, and I'm fairly certain I was too young to be hearing about this level of carnage.

In Canada, November 11 is Remembrance Day. Every year in school there was a minute of silence honouring "Our glorious dead." People wore poppies on their lapels in reference to the poem "In Flanders Fields" by the Canadian poet John McCrae. The poem was read over the PA system.

IN FLANDERS FIELDS

In Flanders fields the poppies blow
Between the crosses, row on row,
That mark our place; and in the sky
The larks, still bravely singing, fly
Scarce heard amid the guns below.

We are the Dead. Short days ago
We lived, felt dawn, saw sunset glow,
Loved and were loved, and now we lie
In Flanders fields.

Take up our quarrel with the foe:
To you from failing hands we throw
The torch; be yours to hold it high.
If ye break faith with us who die
We shall not sleep, though poppies grow
In Flanders fields.

That poem scared the shit out of me. And I guess it probably should have.

The purpose of Remembrance Day is to honour our veterans, but it's really about death. In America, they've parsed out one day for veterans and one for those who have made the ultimate sacrifice (Memorial Day). In Canada, we're sort of all about the dead part.

November 11 is also my brother Paul's birthday. Consequently, Paul is particularly prone to Canadian morbidity. Any time we drove past traffic accidents, Paul had the unnatural fear, even at the age of seven, that our car would be commandeered and turned into a "makeshift ambulance." He specifically feared that he would be saddled with a "headless corpse." I am not making this up.

One time, there was a plane crash at the Toronto airport. From our apartment balcony we could see a plume of smoke in the distance. We saw from the news that bodies from that crash were being stored in a hockey rink across from the crash site. We found that particularly frightening. At that moment, there was a knock at our door. Paul screamed, "Don't answer it! It could be somebody asking us to turn our apartment into a makeshift morgue."

Toronto is blessed with one of the greatest children's hospitals in the world. Despite the fact that they perform miracles every day, this hospital has a remarkably morbid name: The Hospital for Sick Children. My American friends don't even believe me when I tell them it's called the Hospital for Sick Children—I always have to go online to prove it to them. They're horrified. They say to me, "Isn't it obvious that if the children are in the hospital, they're sick? Can't they change the name?"

And I say, "They have changed the name. They've shortened it. It's now called SickKids." Once again, I have to go online to prove it to them.

There is another fantastic yet morbidly named Canadian organization that gathers money for Canadian soldiers who have lost limbs. It's called the War Amps. American friends ask, "What's an 'amp'?" I explain that it's a short form for *amputee*, to which they recoil and say, "So, you guys shortened the word *amputee* down to *amp*?"

"Yes," I say.

"Couldn't it be called something like the Canadian Wounded War Veterans Association? Did they need to have the word *amputee* in the name?" they ask.

And I politely respond, "Yes, they did."

Even Canadian sports can be morbid. American football teams win the Super Bowl. Canadian football teams play for the Grey Cup. That's right: the Grey Cup.

But I think the best example of our obsession with all things morbid is to be found in our cinema. In many ways, the Canadian movie industry is merely an adjunct of the American movie industry. Americans make movies in Canada to take advantage of our tax breaks and our devalued currency, earning the Canadian film community the nickname Hollywood North. I don't think this name is accurate. When Canadians make movies about Canada, our movies tend to be a little morbid. Whereas I like the nickname Hollywood North, I think a more apt name for the Canadian film industry is Cinema Bleak. Our movies deal with

TV Home

Les Troubbes de Johnny

→ A young man who loves costumes experiences a series of setbacks. As his wife left him, he goes after her to live some rather funny adventures.

Watch

MORE   MORE

Movies Canadian

Bang Bang Baby

→ A teen believes her dream of becoming famous will come true when her idol gets stranded in town. A leak in a chemical plant turns her dream into a nightmare. (90 min)

Preview   Watch

MORE   MORE

tragedy in a way that would even make Swedes say, "Come on, Canada, lighten up."

The classic Canadian film *Goin' Down the Road*, released in 1970, is about two naive Bluenosers (Nova Scotians) headed to Toronto. An abridged Wikipedia description of the plot reads as follows: Pete and Joey drive from Nova Scotia to Toronto with the hope of finding jobs. They find minimum-wage jobs at $2 an hour. They turn their "good fortune" into a small apartment, where Joey decides to marry his now-pregnant girlfriend, Betty. His debt-driven lifestyle strains his finances. Pete and Joey get laid off. Unable to find work, with bills to pay and a baby on the way, they get caught stealing food from a supermarket on Christmas Eve. Then they pawn their colour TV and head west, leaving Betty and her unborn child in Toronto. Wow. Deeee-pressing.

The IMDB logline for the Canadian film *Wedding in White* (1972) reads as follows: "A father will do anything to protect his family's reputation when his unmarried teenage daughter becomes pregnant because she was raped by her brother's friend." *Super* deeee-pressing.

The 1981 David Cronenberg film *Scanners* is slightly more upbeat. It's a science fiction film about a man with unbelievable psychic powers who has the ability

to make other people's heads explode. The movie contains perhaps the most graphic head explosion since Abraham Zapruder's 1963 film chronicling the Kennedy assassination.

The 1996 film *Crash* explores the world of "auto-eroticism," wherein severely disturbed, numbed-out people can only get sexually aroused by being in car accidents. It's a great film that plays on the old formula of boy meets girl, boy loses girl, boy gets girl into a car

that goes over the guardrail, boy gets girl back in ICU. You know, that old chestnut. It's dark. Fascinating, but dark.

But perhaps the greatest example of Cinema Bleak is Atom Egoyan's 1997 film *The Sweet Hereafter*. Though based on an American novel, it took a Canadian to bring this so, so, so, *so* bleak story to a cinema near you. Wikipedia describes the plot of *The Sweet Hereafter* in the following way: "In a small town in British Columbia, a school bus skids into a lake, killing fourteen children. The grieving parents are approached by a lawyer, Mitchell Stephens (Ian Holm), who is haunted by his dysfunctional relationship with his drug-addict daughter. Stephens persuades the reluctant parents to file a class-action lawsuit against the state, school district, or other entity for damages, arguing that the accident is a result of negligence.

"The case depends on the few surviving witnesses to say the right things in court; particularly Nicole

Burnell, a fifteen-year-old now paralyzed from the waist down. Before the accident, Nicole was an aspiring songwriter and was being sexually abused by her father, Sam (Tom McCamus).

"One bereaved parent, Billy Ansel, distrusts Stephens and pressures Sam to drop the case; Nicole overhears their argument. In the pretrial deposition, Nicole unexpectedly accuses the bus driver Dolores Driscoll (Gabrielle Rose) of speeding, halting the lawsuit. Stephens and Nicole's father know she is lying but can do nothing. Two years later, Stephens sees Driscoll working as a bus driver in a city."

I would have loved to have been at the pitch session for this film.

STUDIO EXECUTIVE: Hey, guys, what have you got for us?

FILMMAKERS: It's a movie about a town in B.C.

STUDIO EXECUTIVE: B.C.? I love B.C.! I went fly fishing there two summers ago. What happens?

FILMMAKERS: Well, it's winter. And a school bus full of children crashes into a frozen lake.

STUDIO EXECUTIVE: I love it! So, it's a race to save these kids?

FILMMAKERS: Well, no. Fourteen of the children die immediately.

STUDIO EXECUTIVE: Oh . . . Do any of the kids live?

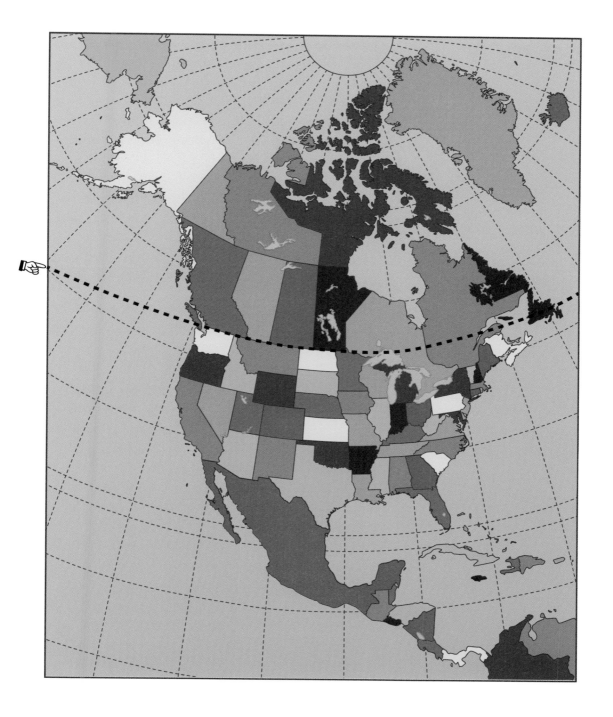

FILMMAKERS: A few, and we focus on one of them. She's an aspiring songwriter.

STUDIO EXECUTIVE: A songwriter! I see where you're going with this, fantastic! She has a song in her heart, and she's finally going to have a chance to sing it!

FILMMAKERS: Unfortunately, she's paralyzed from the waist down.

STUDIO EXECUTIVE: Oh. But at least her parents are happy that she's alive.

FILMMAKERS: Yeah, except that before the accident she was being sexually abused by her father.

STUDIO EXECUTIVE: Gentlemen, I don't like it . . . I LOVE IT!!! I think we have the feel-good hit of the summer.

The Sweet Hereafter is actually a fantastic film. It was nominated for two Academy Awards (Best Director and Best Adapted Screenplay), and it won the Grand Prize of the Jury at the Cannes Film Festival. But let's be frank here: she's paralyzed from the waist down *and* her dad molested her? Well played, Cinema Bleak, well played.

Another way to look at the question of who we are is to point out who we are not.

We are not American.

To talk about Canada without talking about the

"You-Know-Whos" just south of us would be, as we say in Canada, "a bit mental." Pierre Trudeau once said, "Living next to [America] is in some ways like sleeping with an elephant. No matter how friendly and even-tempered is the beast, if I can call it that, one is affected by every twitch and grunt."

I like to think of the relationship between Canada and the United States as that of two brothers.

We both share the same mother, Britain.

Canada and the United States grew up in the same house, North America.

The United States left home as a teenager and became a movie star. Canada decided to stay home and live with Mother.

But why did we decide to stay home? Why didn't Canada join the American Revolution in 1776?

The answer illustrates the fundamental distinctions between Canada and America.

During the American Revolution, some seventy thousand American colonists did not want to split with Britain. Instead, these American refuseniks, who later became known as United Empire Loyalists, chose to move to Canada because they saw the American Revolution not as a story of salvation, but merely as a mercantile-class tax revolt.

The Loyalists agreed that reforms needed to be made, but they were skeptical of this shiny new object called American democracy. This skepticism came from the fact that British colonists were already familiar with democracy—*parliamentary* democracy—going back some five hundred years to the Magna Carta. The

I LIKE TO THINK OF THE RELATIONSHIP BETWEEN CANADA AND THE UNITED STATES AS THAT OF TWO BROTHERS.

37

British Petition of Right of 1628 had already guaranteed the sanctity of private property, and the British Bill of Rights of 1689 had established rules of search and seizure and granted citizens the right to bear arms. Democracy wasn't new to them; they just wanted to stay within the system and have the system evolve. The Loyalists were not revolutionaries, they were *evolutionaries*, and the effect of their sudden and substantial influx to Canada can still be felt on the Canadian psyche today.

Canadians have much respect for the American Revolution and the framers of their constitution.

Girl Guide cookies
11 oz...312 g

However, some Canadians are mildly amused when those on the extreme right refer to "the framers" as if they were spacemen who landed in America with extraterrestrial knowledge, and not the progressive, intellectual, English human beings they actually were. The extent to which some Americans endow the framers of their constitution with superpowers illustrates America's ability to fashion creation myths so strongly that even I, as a Canadian child, believed that democracy and freedom had never existed before 1776. But then again, in the 1960s and 1970s I learned American history from *The Brady Bunch* and *Bewitched*.

The only time Canada and America came close to becoming the same country was during the War of 1812, which, as I mentioned, Canada won. The War of 1812 was, in many ways, Canada's War of Independence.

While Canada and America did not become one country, we became like two brothers who live in the same duplex. The Canadians have the drafty top floor, the Americans have the preferred ground floor, the fun floor, so fun that they often forget that somebody lives upstairs (us).

Every country has certain people who are visionaries, who have the gift to make things. Often, these people are called strivers. In America, these strivers are celebrated—Thomas Edison, the Wright brothers, Steve Jobs, etc. In Canada, we have no tradition for cultivating, protecting, and ultimately celebrating our strivers. It's true that much attention is given to Frederick Banting and Charles Best, the two Canadian scientists who invented synthetic insulin, but that's the exception that proves the rule. It's almost as if Canadian schools should have a strivers' ed. program. This is a fundamental difference between Canada and America.

Not everybody has to be a striver. Canada does a very good job of trying to raise the standard of living of all its citizens. I think this is admirable and appropriate. However, those poor, tortured Canadian souls who are driven to innovate and make things don't just have to endure the typical loneliness of genius, they also must overcome the inertia of a culture that continually asks strivers, "Who do you think you are?"

There is a sociological concept called the competence-deviance hypothesis, which states that people will overlook the deviant behaviour of an artist in proportion to how successful they are. To put it colloquially, "Sure, he looks crazy, but who am I to judge his deviant behaviour because, look, he's successful." The hypothesis goes further. It says that people don't just tolerate the

39

artist's deviant behaviour, they believe that the artist's success *is because of* the deviant behaviour.

Canada has no patience for the competence-deviance hypothesis. At the first sign of deviance, Canadians will tend to devalue even the most gifted person's work, as if the deviant behaviour makes the work an ill-gotten gain.

There's a word for people who need talent and normalcy to be congruent, and that word is *provincial*. Other countries have the tall poppy syndrome, but theirs has more to do with jealousy, whereas Canada's tall poppy syndrome has more to do with an almost Calvinistic disdain for the flamboyant and the excessive. Because Canada is one of the most blessed, educated, peaceful, and tolerant countries in the world, I have great faith that the next generation of Canadians might very well be the first to abandon the tall poppy syndrome. We will go from "Who do you think you are?" to "Who do you want to be?" Imagine the explosion of creativity that would come from that.

I hope Canada will soon stop looking to others for validation. I grew up hearing over and over again that this or that was "Canada's answer to . . . whatever" and that "whatever" was usually something American. The problem with "Canada's answer to . . ." is that nobody's asking. Canadian Paul Anka was not Canada's answer to Frank Sinatra. Have you ever heard an American say that someone was "America's answer" to anything?

Canadians complain about how hard it is to make culture, living next to the cultural powerhouse of the United States. I've always thought this was ironic. Surely

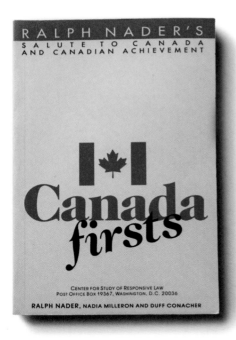

it's an advantage to be close to the culture that not only invented but mastered filmed entertainment. We should study American film production with the same fervour that martial arts students study Japanese masters. Los Angeles is the best place on the planet to make filmed entertainment. It's not just Canadians who go down there; the whole world goes there. Even the Soviet filmmaker Eisenstein agreed that American movies were superior. The Englishmen Alfred Hitchcock, David Lean, Adrian Lyne, and Ridley Scott all made movies in America, as did the Pole Roman Polanski, not to mention the Austrian Otto Preminger. Ang Lee made *The Ice Storm*, portraying American type-A personalities, despite having grown up in Taipei.

Perhaps because we live next door to America, we wait for Hollywood to knock on our door instead of making our own movies about our own lives. We shouldn't wait to be hired. We should just hire ourselves. We shouldn't wait for Broadway, we should make our own stage. It's been said that theatre is merely two planks and a passion. If that's the case, then go to Canadian Tire and buy two planks. We shouldn't wait to be "discovered." We should discover ourselves.

We should be our own cultural engineers. The difference between an engineer and a physicist is that the engineer doesn't need to have done all his "proving math" before he begins building. Americans don't wait for the "proving math." Canadians often mistakenly believe that a flow chart of design must include a box called "foolproof" before we go into action. We're failure-phobic. Americans are not. In fact, NASA doesn't use the F-word; instead, they call failure "early

WE SHOULDN'T WAIT TO BE "DISCOVERED." WE SHOULD DISCOVER OURSELVES.

attempts at success." Canadians need to embrace the concept of "You'll see it when you believe it," and while there will be rejections, we should let the rejections inform us and not define us.

America is comfortable with achievement. Canada less so. I feel that this is a result of Canada not having a clear mission statement. It affects our confidence and it starts in a Canadian childhood.

Canadians are at a disadvantage when it comes to describing their childhood. There are no movies about growing up in Canada to which we can point as a shorthand. English people have *Lord of the Flies*, *Harry Potter*, *Mary Poppins*, or even *Bend It Like Beckham*. Americans have . . . anything by Disney. Canadians, on the other hand, got nothin'. Therefore, when I try to describe my Canadian childhood, I often feel like I'm describing a dream I had.

Try explaining to a non-Canadian *The Friendly Giant*. Or *Mr. Dressup*. Or Danny Gallivan. Or Howie Meeker. Or Stompin' Tom. Or Don Cherry. Or Lanny McDonald. Or Eddie Shack. Or Cherry Lolas. Or the Food Building. Or the PNE. Or Le bonhomme de neige. Or Luba. Or *The Forest Rangers*. Or the Calgary Stampede. Or Dildo, Newfoundland. Or Lotta Hitschmanova. Or the Roughriders, and then, of course, the Rough Riders. Or St. Johns and St. John.

It was all a dream. . . . Or was it?

CHAPTER TWO

A Canadian Childhood

I WAS BORN IN TORONTO, Canada, on May 25, 1963, the youngest of three boys. My parents, Bunny and Eric Myers, came to Canada in 1956 from Liverpool, England. England had won the war but lost the peace, and in the mid-1950s England's number 1 export was young people looking for jobs. Family legend has it that my dad was actually in Canada as a stepping stone to moving to Buffalo, New York. My dad had been a rubber technician for Dunlop Tires in Liverpool, and there was a Dunlop Tire factory in Tonawanda, just outside of Buffalo. Supposedly, he went there to show up for work, but there was no job. And hey presto, I'm a Canuck.

I'm British by heritage, American by God's grace, and Canadian by divine intervention.

45

These are my parents in Liverpool, getting on the boat to come to Canada in 1956. Note the Mersey Docks and Harbour gangway.

There's no one more English than an Englishman who no longer lives in England. And my working-class Liverpudlian father never got over missing England. When he arrived in Canada, the Canadian immigration official said, "The problem with you limeys is that you come over here and think you can change this country. You can't change Canada. Canada will change you." In fact, Canada never did change my dad. It didn't even make a dent.

Our apartment in Toronto looked like a set from the long-running English soap opera *Coronation Street*. Weird wallpaper, Liverpool knickknacks, a ceramic penguin on the TV, paintings of Spaniards whose eyes followed you around the room, miniaturized brass and leather bridle bits, and many portraits of Her Majesty the Queen.

My parents never missed one of the Queen's speeches on Christmas Day. My dad, ever loyal to Britain, loved Prime Minister John Diefenbaker because "Dief the Chief" wanted to keep the original Canadian flag (Red Ensign) that had the Union Jack in the upper left canton. My dad was so English that he even held a grudge against the Hawaiian people,

Her Majesty Queen Elizabeth II

because in 1779 the Hawaiian natives killed the English explorer Captain James Cook. My dad would seethe as if it had happened yesterday and not some two hundred years earlier. "The bloody Hawaiians murdered him, mate. In his sleep!" As though murdering somebody in their sleep compounds the severity of the crime and casts extra aspersions on a murderer's character. "In his bloody sleep, mate! Murdered!" We couldn't have pineapples in the house. "Get that bloody pineapple out of here. Bloody Hawaiians. Those poi-eating, grass skirt–wearing, outrigger canoe–making murderers."

My parents made no concessions to the fact that they were now living in Canada. They continued to use English-isms, often getting incensed when Canadians didn't understand what a flannel is (face cloth), what a lift is (elevator), or what a lorry is (truck). My mum insisted on calling the Toronto Maple Leafs

In fact, "Toronto Maple Leafs" is grammatically correct, and not a long uncorrected mistake as my mother would have Canada believe. Stephen Pinker, in his book *The Language Instinct*, says, "As for the Maple Leafs, the noun being pluralized is not leaf, the unit of foliage, but a noun based on the name Maple Leaf, Canada's national symbol. A name is not the same thing as a noun . . . Therefore, the noun a Maple Leaf (referring to, say, the goalie) must be headless, because it is a noun based on a word that is not a noun. And a noun that does not get its nounhood from one of its components cannot get an irregular plural from that component either; hence it defaults to the regular form Maple Leafs." Got that?

the Toronto Maple *Leaves*, as if Canadians didn't realize the grammatical mistake, and as if my mother's constant correction would make "them" finally see the error of "their" ways. "They" were the Canadians. My brothers and I often had to point out that "they" were us.

My dad made fun of my "horrible" Canadian accent. At dinner, I would say, "Hey, Dad, pass the sauce." My father would wince, as if nails had been scratched on a chalkboard, and would mimic me saying, "Saaaass" in my accent, grotesquely exaggerating the flat *A* of the Canadian dialect. Then he would say, "D'ya hear that, Missus? 'Saaaass' for *sauce*. Can you believe our kids have this terrible accent?" To which my brother Peter would reply, "You're the one with the accent, limey freak! You're the foreigner. You're in Canada." My dad would mutter, "Unfortunately. Watch it, mate, you're going the right way for a smacked bottom. I'll give you a proper go-along." A go-along is a smack so hard that it makes you go along down the street. And what's with "proper"? Is there an "improper" go-along? Freaks.

My dad's refusal to accept that he lived in another country even extended to the Miss Universe pageant. Each nation's contestant would come out in alphabetical order. Canada came out before the United Kingdom, in either the Cs or the Ds (depending upon whether we were called the Dominion of Canada or just Canada). My brothers and I would cheer for Miss Canada. My dad would often make barking sounds—insinuating that Miss Canada was a "dog." Every year, he arbitrarily claimed that Miss United Kingdom was prettier than Miss Canada, saying of Miss Canada, "Don't care for yours much, mate. I've seen better legs on a piano. I'll give you this much: she's got a great face for radio."

In many ways, I'm as Canadian as I am because I was constantly defending Canada's honour.

In my own house.

In Canada.

Perhaps my limey dad was the necessary pessimist who helped me forge my Canadian identity. My parents would often joke that they came to Canada to make money, but ended up making kids instead. My dad, a child of the Depression, was obsessed with the technology of thrift. He spent so much money trying to save money. I sometimes wished he had applied the same amount of energy to the technology of wealth, but ultimately, my dad believed that having a sense of humour was more important than having money.

The Beatles sang, "I don't care too much for money / Money can't buy me love," and in economically depressed Liverpool, Scousers often didn't own anything except their bodies and their sense of humour. My dad wouldn't let anyone into the house if he thought they didn't have a sense of humour. He would say, "Michael, your friend Mark is not welcome in this house anymore."

And I would say, "Why not?"

He would respond, "'Cause he's not funny. In order to come into this house, you have to have at least one good song, one good story, or one good joke."

An example of both my dad's thrift and his love of comedy was when we went to Quebec City in the seventies, at the height of separatist tensions. When you have three little kids on a car trip, you're constantly stopping for bathroom breaks. My father was a British Army veteran who insisted on keeping a schedule

("SHED-youl") so we were instructed to pee into bottles. At one point, I had to pee. My dad said, "I'm not bloody stopping, mate. I have a schedule." But we had run out of bottles, so I had to pee on a pie plate and hold the plate for fifty miles. We finally got to Montreal, pulled off the highway, and came to a stop sign in front of Quebec separatist protestors. My dad shouted, "All right, open the door and dump the pie plate!"

I threw my urine onto the grass in front of the separatists. They were furious. It appeared to them that we had driven all the way from Ontario just to throw our urine at them.

My brother Paul panicked. "They're gonna kill us! Go!"

My dad sped off, yelling, "Keep your heads down!" It was not a great start to the trip.

My dad, in true Liverpool form, refused to pay for a hotel. We camped. Scousers are not great campers, and my dad was so stingy that he refused to pay the nominal fee for a provincial campground. "I'm not paying them bloody prices," which, I'm sure, was the princely sum of two dollars (Canadian) a night. So instead we camped for "free" on government land, sticking it to "the Man" in a swampy bog by the highway. That summer, Canada had been hit with a gypsy moth infestation, and that night in our bog, the Coleman lantern was swarmed by thousands of disgusting moths.

The next morning, my dad got up and made a "breakfast" of instant oatmeal and tea. "All right, get up, you lazy buggers. Come and face the great outdoors." At precisely that moment, we heard the thrum of a low-flying prop plane that dusted our gypsy-moth-infested campsite with a layer of toxic white DDT. The tent, the car, and my dad were covered in it. We ventured out of

51

Eric Myers, my dad, finding something funny. Hopefully.

the tent to see my dad looking like the victim of an unfortunate talcum powder incident, mug of tea in hand, hair now greyed by DDT. Without missing a beat, he said, "All right, how fast can we find this funny?" That was one of my dad's greatest gifts, as well as one of the greatest characteristics of the English: they find things funny quickly. My dad would say, "There's nothing so terrible that can't be laughed at."

In Liverpool, what could be laughed at was yourself. Self-deprecation is a hallmark of English and, by extension, Canadian comedy. The joke's on us. Comedy in Canada and England is a coping mechanism. My dad felt that man's natural state was silly, that humans are only serious so that they can get to their silly. Someone once asked my dad, "Is everything a joke?" To which my dad replied, "Hopefully."

SELF-DEPRECATION IS A HALLMARK OF ENGLISH AND, BY EXTENSION, CANADIAN COMEDY. THE JOKE'S ON US.

It was a John Lennonesque type of comedy. Lots of wordplay, like John's famous quote about whether he would hold a grudge against Nixon: "No, I don't hold a grudge against him. Time wounds all heels." My dad would say things like, "We're never short of a theory in Liverpool. At least that's my theory." And "In a perfect world, you wouldn't need utopias." If we pulled into a stranger's driveway to make a U-turn, he would, without fail, say, "We're here!" and then, "Everyone out, don't give your right name." After a meal, he would say, "If that's my dinner, I've had it." Every time we passed a cemetery, he'd say, "That's the dead centre of Toronto. People are dying to get in there, mate." And if I protested any parental instruction and asked, "Why do I have to do this?" my dad would say, "Because in this play we call life, I play the role of your father, that's why. You play the role of the son. It must be terrible to have no power. I'd rather be me, mate. I've got all the power." He hated to shout; he preferred to joke.

My strongest memories of my father involve me sitting in bed on a school night, hearing him in the living room, laughing at a comedy movie. I would feign annoyance and say, "I have to get up for school tomorrow." My dad would say, "Sit down, this is Peter Sellers. He's a genius. Fancy a cup of tea?" And he would literally keep me awake, because it was important to him that I appreciated humour, especially English humour. There was a ton of comedy in my house. This was always an occasion for a truce. When a comedy was on in our apartment, everything was better—somehow the apartment even smelled better.

Despite his denial, my dad did, in fact, like Canadians. He liked how much they loved comedy. My dad also loved hockey, taking to it the second he got off the boat. He loved the Toronto Maple Leafs (as do I). And even though my dad was a diehard Liverpool FC fan (as am I), my dad saw hockey almost as an "improvement" on soccer. My British relatives would say, "But Eric, football is a thinking man's game." My dad would

53

say, "True, but hockey is a *fast*-thinking man's game."

As much as we loved hockey, neither my brothers nor I played hockey on ice growing up. We couldn't afford it. I played a little bit of shinny, but hockey gear for three boys, for an immigrant family, was just too expensive. Soccer was much cheaper.

The soccer team I played on was called the North York Spartans, which prompted my dad to say, "Didn't the mothers of Sparta send their children out to die?" I played soccer for five glorious seasons, making friendships that I still have, like my teammate and best friend of forty years, David Mackenzie. "Mackenzie," as my family calls him (my dad called him McEnroe—I don't know why), was the unofficial fourth Myers brother. Born in Nottingham, England, Mackenzie came to Canada at the age of four. His family, like mine, were working people, unaccustomed to the finer things in life but cognizant of the important things in life like friendship and laughter. But, Mackenzie, like my brother Paul—and many Canadians—was particularly morbid. His favourite jokes were the "Mommy, Mommy" jokes, like:

"Mommy, Mommy, I'm tired of eating spaghetti . . . "
"Shut up, or I'll rip the veins out of your other arm."

Or the classic:

> "Mommy, Mommy, I'm tired of going around in circles."
> "Shut up or I'll nail your other foot to the floor."

Morbid.

Canada in the 1960s and '70s was a great place to grow up poor. During that time, the social safety net made it so that, while I knew we weren't rich, I didn't feel we were poor. Of course, we never went hungry, unlike my parents, who, during the war in Liverpool, literally ate only one egg a week—the yolk on Tuesday, and the egg white on Saturday. The food shortage forced my father

to join the Royal Engineers in the British Army at the age of fourteen, not because of the gathering storm clouds of war in Europe, but because there literally wasn't enough food for my dad, who was the youngest of seven. His only option was to lie about his age and take the King's coin—and food.

We in Canada were fortunate enough not to have to take such drastic measures. We had universal healthcare, which meant that getting sick never meant extra catastrophe. Plus, we had fantastic schools and a low crime rate. We felt safe and secure. It's one thing to be poor; it's another thing to be poor and feel unsafe. One could say crime is the insult to the injury, but it's really the extra injury to the injury.

Our relative safety allowed us a joyful innocence that can sometimes be mistaken for naiveté. Our favourite things didn't cost money, things like bike hikes, snowball fights, watching storms roll in, television, British bulldog, relievio. My neighbourhood was filled with the song of "Olly olly oxen free!" and, when we played street hockey, "Car!" followed by "Game on!" When we played touch football (with three downs), you would hear kids counting out, "One Manitoba, two Manitoba, three Manitoba . . . ," with the inevitable complaint, "Awfully fast on the Manitobas, eh?" This was no-money fun.

Of course, there were times when my brothers and I were aware that we weren't the Rockefellers. My winter parka was not bought from an Eaton's catalogue but from the discount store Honest Ed's. And the zipper on that knock-off parka never saw a lift ticket—skiing was for Canadians, tobogganing was for us immigrants. Super Slider Snow Skates (whisper: Super Slider Snow Skates) was as close as I got to being Jean-Claude Killy. I never wore Levi's, but instead I wore "Live's," and one luxurious Christmas I got a pair of GWGs. My Adidas—or, more accurately, my "Nadidas"—had four stripes and not the trademark

EATON'S
Fall and Winter 1972

SHOP BY PHONE: For local numbers, see page 887

Your Account Number   Eaton's Telephone Number

SHOPPING SERVICE PAGES, beginning page 881
INDEX page 895

Good values plus convenience-always in season at Eaton's

three stripes of the so-called "legitimate" Adidas sneakers. I'd spend hours trying to remove the fourth stripe, but it left behind a discoloured phantom stripe—a shibboleth of footwear, giving away my working-class identity. (This book was almost called *Canada: My Adidas Had Four Stripes.*)

Occasionally, a parent from one of the "nice houses" in the adjacent subdivision would marvel at my general knowledge, given that I was from, as they put it, the "low rentals." It's not like I lived in "the hood." I cannot claim to have grown up on the "mean streets" of Scarborough. Because even those "mean streets" could be awfully nice and hopeful.

Mackenzie and I, and the North York Spartans Soccer Club that we played for, won many trophies between '73 and '78. I still have those trophies, and they mean as much to me as any award I've ever received. The ethnic makeup of our team reflected the New Canada. There were first-generation British Canadians, West Indian Canadians, East Indian Canadians, and Asian Canadians. We didn't have fancy uniforms; we played for pride.

As a sidebar, I want to mention that my dad never missed one of my soccer games. Even when he had shingles and looked like the Elephant Man, he merely put on sunglasses and a hat and drove me and Mackenzie to the game.

One summer, we played an American team. They showed up in a team bus, almost like a professional team, their team name permanently painted on the side. They had cheerleaders and giant Gatorade coolers. The coach had a whiteboard to illustrate plays and a bullhorn to call out set pieces. Their uniforms were a work of art: red, white, and blue, perfectly matching, names on the back, numbers on the shorts, and matching sock garters. Our uniforms were "red," although orange would suffice, and matching shorts were optional. One Scottish kid played in cutoff jeans.

Our home-field goals were repurposed football uprights that didn't have netting. Not to worry, the Americans had brought spare nets, which their "assistants" fetched from the bus and promptly set up. The Americans finished their synchronized warm-up, changed out of their track suits, got last-minute instructions from the whiteboard, took a knee and prayed (wow), huddled up, and performed an intimidating cheer that would have even scared the mean blond kid from Cobra Kai.

I CANNOT CLAIM TO HAVE GROWN UP ON THE "MEAN STREETS" OF SCARBOROUGH. BECAUSE EVEN THOSE "MEAN STREETS" COULD BE AWFULLY NICE AND HOPEFUL.

We beat them, 10–nil.

Halfway through the second half, at around 6–nil, we had so much confidence, we substituted in our asthmatic players. One kid with a halo brace scored a goal from a corner kick. The American team, a bedraggled and beaten army, returned to their bus. We, however, celebrated by eating Lowney's Glosette Raisins and by playing our team song, "Shattered" by the Rolling Stones, on someone's Fisher-Price Close 'n' Play record player. My dad came over and switched off the music and

IT WAS IMPORTANT
TO WIN, BUT MORE
IMPORTANT WAS HOW
YOU WON. AND IT
DIDN'T MATTER IF WE
WERE PLAYING "RICH"
TEAMS, "POOR" TEAMS,
OR AMERICANS.

made us give a friendly wave to the Americans. He insisted on good sportsmanship. It was important to win, but more important was how you won. And it didn't matter if we were playing "rich" teams, "poor" teams, or Americans.

The Americans, they seemed famous to us. America seemed like a place where anything could happen. In Canada, you can support even the most outrageous claims of deviant human behaviour simply by saying it happened "somewhere in the States, eh?"

For example, "Did you hear about that lady? That would steal babies from the hospital? And raise them? Convincing them that they're deaf?"

"That didn't happen!"

"Yes, it did!"

"Where?"

"Somewhere in the States, eh?"

"Wow, those people are crazy, eh?"

"Right, eh? If I had to live in the States, I'd have to smoke a bag o' dope every day."

Of course, we Canadians frequently envy Americans. I myself was envious of the American Space Program. How come Canada didn't have a rocket? How come Canada didn't have a NASA? And come to think of it, how come Canada didn't even have its own car?

I love American space stuff so much that I remember buying an Airfix model of the Apollo Saturn V rocket. It was three feet tall. I was green with envy that it was

covered in American flags and had UNITED STATES and U.S.A. emblazoned all over it. When I finished the model of the Saturn V rocket, I threw away the American decals, and instead I got a Sharpie and, in my steadiest hand, wrote C A N A D A along the length of the launch vehicle. I found some Canadian-flag stickers and placed them where the American flags should go. Well done, America.

I was also envious of American television. Let's face it: America makes the best TV shows in the world. That's not to say I didn't love *Monty Python's Flying Circus* and other brilliant British shows; it's just, come on: *M*A*S*H*, *The Dick Van Dyke Show*, *The Mary Tyler Moore Show*, *The Bob Newhart Show*, *The Ed Sullivan Show*, *The Rockford Files*, *Hogan's Heroes*, *The Man from U.N.C.L.E.*, *Rod Serling's Night Gallery*, *The Monkees*, *H.R. Pufnstuf*, *The Muppets*, and *Hee Haw*, which featured Canadian Don Harron as his character Charlie Farquharson, the radio newscaster for station KORN, an American station, and yet, to us at home, he had the thickest Canuck accent going. I salute you, Don Harron. I just want to take a second, also, to give a loving shout out to *SCTV*. I'm so proud that they're Canadian. There's a lot of Bob and Doug McKenzie from *SCTV* in *Wayne's World*: both sketches were unabashedly local and had a homemade feel to them. Thank you, *SCTV*. Thank you, Dave Thomas, and thank you, Rick Moranis.

Growing up in Toronto, the local American TV we got was from Buffalo. We got *Bowling for Dollars*,

Hereby officially stated: No Bob and Doug? No Wayne and Garth.

which is pretty self-explanatory; the children's show *Rocketship 7*, which was so low-budget, we owe Canadian TV an apology. But the highlight of Buffalo TV was, of course, the legendary Irv Weinstein.

Irv was the main newscaster for *Eyewitness News* on channel 7. He is a folk hero in Toronto. Ted Baxter-like, yet much smarter and way more tasteful. He was the ultimate anchorman. To us in Toronto, it seemed like Buffalo was constantly on fire. We marvelled at Irv Weinstein's ability to come up with synonyms for firefighters. For example, he could say, "Buffalo fire-fighters today battled a three-alarmer in an abandoned rooming house at Lackawanna and Main." In the next story, it would be, "Buffalo blaze-busters tackled a massive electrical fire in an abandoned factory near Grand Island." Or it could be, "Buffalo smoke-eaters today are still battling an unyielding inferno in an abandoned carpet store in Tonawanda." All the stories ended the same way: "Arson is suspected."

Similarly, it seemed to us in Toronto that there was a twenty-four-hour-a-day running gun battle happening on the streets of Buffalo. When I was old enough to steal beer, we developed a drinking game. Everyone had to take a sip of Molson Export every time Irv Weinstein said, "Arson is suspected" or "The suspect died later of multiple gunshot wounds." On one humid August evening, there were so many fires and gun battles in Buffalo that I almost gave myself alcohol poisoning.

> WE DEVELOPED A DRINKING GAME. EVERYONE HAD TO TAKE A SIP OF MOLSON EXPORT EVERY TIME IRV WEINSTEIN SAID, "ARSON IS SUSPECTED" OR "THE SUSPECT DIED LATER OF MULTIPLE GUNSHOT WOUNDS."

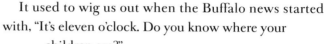

It used to wig us out when the Buffalo news started with, "It's eleven o'clock. Do you know where your children are?"

Up in Canada, we were like, "What's going on? Where are the children? Should we get in a car and go down to Buffalo and help find the children?"

When there was a snowstorm, my brothers and I would watch Buffalo TV and be jealous of Buffalo school children as the newscasters read out the names of schools that were closed because of the snow. We never had snow days! Equally upsetting was Kentucky Fried Chicken. How is it that a state that was one-tenth the size of my province, Ontario, had a dish named after it, especially one that was so delicious that my father claimed it had a chemical in it that made you crave it every two weeks. Equally puzzling was Colonel Sanders. Why was he a colonel? Later, I found out that he was a Kentucky colonel, which is an honorary title. My dad, however, a critic of the Vietnam War, said, "Colonel Sanders? The Americans have even managed to militarize chicken."

It was also a travesty that you would see toys advertised on American TV that were not sold in Canada. And if the toy *was* sold in Canada, the announcer would give the price and then a super-sped-up announcer would tack on, "Canadian orders add ten dollars." Canadian orders add ten dollars? That's not fair! Even less fair was when that same sped-up guy would say, "Not available in Canada." Cruel.

We were obsessed with the Buffalo accent—the way the

Me on Halloween. I went into a supermarket thinking that I wouldn't be recognized in such elaborate makeup. A young lady approached me and said, "You are him, right?" I thought to myself, "How could anyone recognize me? The makeup took me three hours!" Reluctantly I said, "Yes." The lady said, "Mister Colonel Sanders, it is an honour to meet you."

word *top* sounded like "tap." The word *dollar* sounded like "daller." They worshiped "Gad," and they loved their "dyad" and "mawm." I'm sure they would pay "tap daller" to see their "dyad" hanging out with "Gad."

But of course, Canadians have an accent too. Some Canadians think the Canadian accent is, by its nature, the absence of an accent. As if the Canadian accent is zero on any given accent-measurement scale. They are deluded. The Canadian accent has its own vowel sounds, lexicon, and pronunciations. For example, in the Canadian accent, *process* sounds like PROH-sess; *milk* can sound more like melk; *margarine* is pronounced mar-jer-EEN, like wolverine; *tiger* can slip into tagger; decals become deckles. Canadians pronounce New Orleans as New Or-LEENS. In Canada, *pasta* is pronounced paasta, like Mount Shasta, and you'll eat the leftovers to-MORE-oh, not tuh-MARR-ow. Your mother is not your mom, but your mum, and if she's a sex worker, she's not a whore, she's a hoo-er.

> CANADIANS THINK THE CANADIAN ACCENT IS, BY ITS NATURE, THE ABSENCE OF AN ACCENT. THEY ARE DELUDED.

There are a few regional variations in pronunciation, even within Canada. For example, in Vancouver, *dollar* can tend to sound like DOLE-er. In the west, your car would go in the ger-ADJ, which rhymes with *badge*, and the front of a building, the *facade*, would tend to sound like the fis-SAD. In Atlantic Canada, they'll say something is right nice, but it will sound like it's roit noice. If you were on a tour boat, you'd be on a tore boat (though in Vancouver, it would be a two-er boat).

For Canadians, the last letter of the alphabet is not

64

zee but zed. I remember with great affection the first time I saw Zed Zed Top in concert. Years later, I would meet Jay-Zed and we would sit on a Lay-Zed-Boy chair, which I paid for with three E-Zed payments of $49.99.

Then there are some phrases that are uniquely Canadian. In Canada, when you're sick, you're not in *the* hospital, you're just "in hospital."

"Did you hear about Bill? He's in hospital. In front of his kids, eh?"

A knit cap is a *toque*, pronounced "tewk"; a variety store is a smoke and gift; and you're in Grade 8, not the eighth grade. In the States, if you were hooked up, you would say, "I know a guy." In Canada, it's "a buddee o' mine," as in, "A buddee o' mine has some snow tires." In a fight, you don't kick a guy, you *hoof* him—as in "A buddee o' mine got hoofed in the nuts." If you spit on somebody, you *hork* on them; if you step in a puddle, you get a *soaker*; if you suspect that somebody's crazy, you say, "Careful: buddy's mental!" Someone who's a trash-talker has got a *smart mouth*. No one is likely to call you on the phone, but they might phone you and have

a call. Marijuana is often called *smokin' dope*, a twenty-four-pack of beer is a *two-four*, which ends up getting shortened to *tewf*. In Scarborough, a twelve-pack of beer with a built-in handle is called a *Scarborough suitcase*. There is no plural for the word *beer* in Canada. For example, "A buddee o' mine got stopped by the police. They let 'im go, 'cause he'd only had, like, about nine beer."

On a side note, one of the most Canadian things I've ever heard was Joni Mitchell singing, "I could drink a case of you." They

65

should put Joni on the ten-dollar bill.

A penis is often called a *dink*, but a dink is also someone who is ruining all the fun. For example, "There used to be a shortcut to the lake through that fence, but some dink called the cops and now we gotta go all the way around." A common medical condition in Canada is "lake dink." It's the shrinkage that occurs when a male swims in a cold lake. All the lakes in Canada are cold.

A *Newfie* is someone from Newfoundland. Newfoundland joined Canada in 1949, the last province to do so. Newfies are my favourite people in the world. They love to laugh, they love music, and they love hockey. Where does it get bad? Newfoundland is an island off the east coast of Canada, and like all island cultures . . . the residents can be strange. For example, Newfies have an expression for being at home with your socks half on and half off, which they call *Sunday feet*. Why? Similarly, if you choke, something got caught in your *Sunday throat*. I don't know why. In Newfoundland, they have a very unique dialect—very Irish, a little Scottish. There's a famous song written in the Newfie dialect called "I's the B'y," which means "I'm the boy."

I's de b'y dat builds de boat
(I am the boy who builds boats)

And I's de b'y dat sails 'er
(And I am the boy who sails them)

I's de b'y dat catches the fesh
(I am the boy who catches fish)

An' brings dem home to Lizer
(And brings them home to Liza)

Another strange quirk of Newfoundland, and of all of Atlantic Canada, is the linguistic anomaly known as "ingressive pulmonic speech." Basically, people in the Maritimes suck air in quickly when they say the word *yeah*. Try saying *yeah* while breathing in, instead of breathing out. Supposedly, Swedes do this as well. I thought there was an asthma epidemic the first time I went to Newfoundland.

THERE ARE OTHER LINGUISTIC ANOMALIES THAT ONLY EXIST IN A CANADIAN SITUATION.

There are other linguistic anomalies that only exist in a Canadian situation. For example, if you're in a line for a water fountain and someone ahead of you is taking a long time, you'll often hear, "Hey, buddy, hurry up. Don't drink Canada Dry." In Canada, we have bilingual packaging, with both French and English on the same label. When I was a kid, I thought "grape raisin" was a flavour, when in fact, *raisin* is French for "grape." Similarly, I thought "cherry cerise" was also a flavour, and of course, *cerise* is French for "cherry." I thought there was "old fort cheese," when *fort* is French for "strong," which is the equivalent of "old." I only figured this out at the age of seventeen, when I asked someone where the "old fort" was. And when one "cuts the cheese," often you would simply say, "Did you cut? 'Cause it smells cuttish in here." However, the Canadian dialect is evolving. A delineation can be made between the dialects of a young Canadian and an old Canadian. The

Canadian actor Michael Cera has a young Canadian dialect. Elements of the old Canadian dialect can be heard in Bob and Doug McKenzie's "Great White North" sketches on *SCTV*. The old Canadian dialect in its purest form can be heard in Stompin' Tom Connors's accent.

Stompin' Tom Connors was a legendary Canadian folk singer, somewhere between Johnny Cash and Pete Seeger. He kept time by stomping the stage with his boot, so much so that a plywood board had to be placed on the stage to protect it. As an homage, let's name the old Canadian dialect the Stompin' Tom. The Stompin' Tom has its own pronunciations, lexicon, phrases, and jokes.

A Stompin' Tom would pronounce the word *again* as a-GAIN; he would refer to his wife as Mother; his dinner is his supper; Saturday is "Sa-ur-day," and if something happened on a Saturday, it happened on "*the* Sa-ur-day." They're likely to call the supermarket a chain store—not a place where you buy chains but a chain of stores. They will often refer to the hardware store Canadian Tire as Crappy Tire, not because they don't like Canadian Tire (because all Canadians love Canadian Tire) but because older Canadians, like their British antecedents, enjoy complaining for sport, and they are happiest when writing a letter of complaint. The snow tires they buy at Crappy Tire will simply be called "snows," as in, "Mother told me at supper on the Sa-ur-day that there's gonna be a big storm on the Sun-dee, so I better put on the snows that I got from Crappy Tire."

To the Stompin' Tom, snow tires are a form of currency. You can pay people for things in snow tires; as cigarettes are to prisons, so snows are to Stompin' Toms. Stompin' Tom's rear end, he'll call his *arse*. If he likes something a lot, he likes it "sumtin' fierce." When he goes into a Tim Hortons doughnut shop, which he calls Timmy's, he'll get a *double double*—two sugars and two creams. With his double double, he'll probably get a *cruller*, which looks, ironically, like a snow tire. He will call someone from Saskatchewan a *Skatcher*. If he thinks you're being offensive, he'll tell you to *'marten up*, and if he feels you don't understand it, he'll *'splain* it to you. If he's worried that something is volatile, he's concerned it might *'splode*. He might kick your arse till you 'marten up, as he 'splains to you that you're not 'sposa do that cause that thing's gonna 'splode.

If you went to the store to buy cigarettes for him, he is likely to say to you, "Hey, buddy, can you run to the 'moke 'n' gift and get me a deck o' 'mokes?"

If he's mad at you, he'll tell you to go piss up a rope. He calls masturbation "pullin' the goalie." He calls going to the cinema "goin' to the show," but going to a strip show is described as "goin' to the peelers." So he might say, "Go piss up a rope and get your arse over to the show, and avoid goin' to the peelers, 'cause I know you have a tendency to pull the goalie."

If you pee next to a Stompin' Tom at a urinal, he'll always tell you, "This is where the pricks hang out," he'll point out that "the joke is in your hands," and as you finish urinating, he'll remind you that "more than two shakes and you're jackin' off." If you come in with new trousers, he'll call them *slacks* and say, "I had a pair of slacks like that, an' then my mum got a job." He'll ask you, "Hey, buddy, do those slacks come in men's sizes?"

Steaks are always "yay thick." A middle-aged Canadian man's gut is a *Molson muscle* or a *boiler*. And, without fail, he will tell a Classic Old Canadian Guy Joke: "Why do Canadians like to do it doggy style? Because that way they can both watch the hockey game." Truthfully, the Old Canadian would not say "the hockey game"; instead, he would say "the game." The great Canadian goalie Ken Dryden, a true Renaissance man, wrote the definitive book about the game of hockey, simply called *The Game*. Is there any other game?

My favourite Canadian of all time who had a Stompin' Tom accent was Mr. Glenn Cochrane of CFTO-TV News in Toronto. Glenn Cochrane was a community-events reporter. As was often the case with many presenters on Canadian television, being telegenic was not necessarily a prerequisite. In America, the men have always been six feet tall, lantern-jawed, with a full head of protein-depletive hair and a gleaming grille of perfect white teeth. They speak in dulcet tones, free from speech impediments. Not so much in Canada. Glenn had the thickest Stompin' Tom accent, with shushy *S*s, as in "shuffering shuccatash." He had inexpert microphone technique, wore corrective lenses, and his suits looked like they had been washed in Lake Ontario. He

Mr. Glenn Cochrane of CFTO-TV News (with lovely councillor Kay Gardiner). A great Canadian.

was a study in Canadian affect: frozen, stiff, with a repetitive monotone sing-song. Even when he was in his thirties, he seemed like he was in his sixties. I got the sense that he must have said the following sentence at least once in his life: "All right, which one of you jokers hit my kid?" His patter for any given report was identical. It was almost like a Mad Lib, where values were plugged into his pre-written script. Here is an example of a Glenn Cochrane report, from the Sportsmen's Show in Toronto:

> Here we are in Toronto, Ontario, at the Shportshmen's Show. There'sh plenty to do at the Shportshmen's Show, whether you're into fly-fishing or shkeet shooting. Over there ish a thoushand-pound bull, made entirely out of butter. But wherever you go at the Shportshmen's Show . . .
>   *[enter two bikini-clad girls]*
> . . . you're never too far from a coupla lovely ladiesh. Glenn Cochrane, at the Shportshmen's Show, CFTO [pronounced shee-eff-tee-oh] Newsh.

Had Glenn been covering the Chernobyl nuclear disaster, his copy would have read as follows:

> Here we are at Chernobyl, shene of the world'sh worsht nuclear dishashter. There'sh plenty to do at Chernobyl, whether you're meashuring radiation or checking for shoresh. Over there ish a million-pound boron sarcophagush, made entirely out of butter. But wherever you go at Chernobyl . . .

[enter two Russian girls]
. . . you're never too far from a coupla lovely ladiesh. Glenn Cochrane, at Chernobyl, CFTO Newsh."

Glenn Cochrane was such a big part of my life in Toronto. I had the honour of meeting him when he interviewed me in 1993. I did my Glenn Cochrane for Glenn Cochrane. He loved it. I loved him.

The "song" of the Canadian dialect is referred to by linguists as the Canadian rise. In the Canadian accent, there is a tonal rise at the end of each sentence, until the last sentence, which returns to the Canadian monotone. The rise at the end of the sentence is an indication that the speaker intends to continue. The end of the final sentence has no rise, which tells the listener, "Now it's your turn to speak." Here's an example of a Canadian talking, wherein the text in superscript represents the rise in the speaker's intonation:

CANADIAN: A buddy of ^{mine}. [*Still talking*]
Went to Canadian ^{Tire}. [*Still talking*]
And he bought a hockey stick. [*Your turn to talk*]

Essentially, we Canadians have encoded "after you" into our speech patterns—it's subliminal etiquette.

The Canadian accent is not famous. Usually, people only know that Canadians tend to say "eh?" at the ends of their sentences. *Eh* is a bid for affirmation, even for the most banal of statements. For example:

CANADIAN: Dogs are furry, eh?

The logo on the side of this Canadian government train is called the Canada Wordmark. The word "Canada" in this typeface with the flag over the final "a" is trademarked and is an official designation. This was an offshoot of what I call "The Next Great Nation" era.

By placing *eh* at the end of the non-controversial statement "Dogs are furry," the speaker is compelling his listener to affirm the truth of this, as if to say, "Dogs are furry . . . I'm correct in that assessment, right?"

Another Canadianism is that we pronounce *been* as "bean" (they do this in England as well). In America, it's pronounced "bin." I'm often mocked for saying "bean," to which I answer, "When you've seen something, you haven't 'sin' it." Americans don't find this a terribly compelling argument. My American dialect coach for the movie *54*, in which I played Steve Rubell, who was from Queens, had to correct my Canadian pronunciation of *been* so much that he referred to himself as a "bean counter."

Every country has a resting face, a national affect. In *The Labryinth of Solitude*, the Mexican poet Octavio Paz talked about the Mexican affect, describing it as stoic, yet with a servile hostility, pretending to see nothing, but seeing everything, pretending to judge no one, but judging everyone.

Of course, Canada has a national resting face. In the Canadian affect, Canadian men display very little facial mobility, unlike their American counterparts, whose faces are mobile and engaged, almost over-connecting to their words. Canadian men have a frozen affect. The American affect conveys "Look at me, I'm here!" For the Canadian, it conveys "I don't want to show off." Canadian men have a disproportionate fear of being perceived as "conceited." American men harbour no such fear. Instead, Canadians tend to have what Andrew H. Malcolm describes as a "superior inferiority complex."

The Canadian affect for women is very different. Canadian women tend to have a look of mild surprise, a doe-like, exaggeratedly open countenance. The expression equivalent of showing your hands to prove that you have no weapons. In tandem with this non-threatening affect, Canadian women will often inject a sing song-y "Oh yeah" between your sentences. The intention is to clearly communicate, "I want to let you know that I am listening." But to the American ear, this lilting "Oh yeah" sounds like a super-condescending version of "Will you stop talking?" or "Seriously, do I have to listen to this?"

When I was six, my best friend in my building was named Kori Skinner, and his dad was Brian Skinner, a disc jockey on CHUM (the call letters of Canadian TV and radio stations all begin with the letter *C*). CHUM played Top Forty music and had a weekly promotional printout of, infuriatingly, the top *thirty* hits called the CHUM Chart. My brother Paul collected CHUM Charts religiously, and he still has all of them from 1970 and 1971. CHUM had a promotion wherein, if they randomly called you and you answered, "I listen to CHUM," you got a thousand dollars. For my dad, this was his ticket to moving back to Britain. Without fail, he always answered the phone, "I listen to CHUM." One day, a group of neighbours had gathered in our apartment because one of our fellow tenants had passed away. Tears were flowing. Then the phone rang.

My mum knew my dad wanted to win that money, so she said, "Don't answer it, Eric." But he couldn't help himself. As one person was telling a heart-wrenching story of our dearly departed neighbour, my dad picked up the phone and said, as quietly as he could, "I listen to CHUM." He did not win, but it did make everyone laugh. CHUM was "our" station, and even now, when my brother Paul calls, I have been known to answer, "I listen to CHUM." Paul has always joked that the "I listen to CHUM" campaign was so successful that, at that time, even if you had called a suicide hotline they would've answered, "I listen to CHUM. Suicide Hotline. How can I help?"

One day, Kori Skinner said that his dad was going to mention our names on the radio. We waited nervously on the balcony with the radio at full blast. It was one of those muggy early evenings in June where it seems like it's never going to become nighttime and it's so hot that even the cicadas are still making noise. At 6:05 p.m., Brian Skinner said, "I just want to send a special hello to two of the coolest cats in Don Mills: Kori and Mike."

Kori took it in stride. I screamed. This was what I thought being famous felt like. It wasn't until much later—2002, to be precise—that I truly came to know what being famous felt like.

This is what being famous actually feels like.

In 2002, I was coming home from Madison Square Garden, having watched the Leafs lose to the Rangers. I'd eaten everything that MSG had to offer: popcorn, hot dogs, nachos, everything. We shall refer to this as "my first mistake."

In the cab on the way home, I started to get the familiar warning signs of an impending diarrhea attack: the gurgling sound, shooting pains in the front of my legs, and a sweaty brow. I made deals with my body that if it would just let me crap my pants the second I got out of the cab, I would perform various saintly deeds. But my body didn't want to make a deal. It was go time. When the cab came to a stop sign, I threw the cabby a twenty, thus giving him the greatest tip of his life. And this is where I can illustrate the unique experience surrounding the frenzy of renown. As I bolted down the stairs to use a restaurant's bathroom, I was recognized by a young, overly effusive fan.

AND THIS IS WHERE I CAN ILLUSTRATE THE UNIQUE EXPERIENCE SURROUNDING THE FRENZY OF RENOWN.

EFFUSIVE FAN: Mike Myers?! I'm such a big fan! Can I shake your hand?

ME: [*through diarrhea quiver voice*] Not a good time!

I ran down the stairs. The Effusive Fan *followed*! This was going to be bad. I bolted into the bathroom. Unfortunately, it was a single-toilet, single-urinal men's room. It combined the worst of both worlds: small and public. The walls of the stall didn't reach the floor, which is often the case in public bathrooms (why?). In fact, the bottoms of the stall walls were particularly high, at almost knee level, affording little to no privacy. I was about to afford myself some relief when the Effusive Fan decided to *enter the tiny bathroom.*

EFFUSIVE FAN: Mr. Myers, I'm such a big fan. I just really want to shake your hand.

ME: [*high-pitched*] Kinda busy!

EFFUSIVE FAN: That's OK, I'll wait.

He'll wait?! What? So, there I was, exposed, in the down-and-locked position, using all of the telepathy that I don't have to will this person to *leave the bathroom.* There was going to be an explosion. It was going to be bad.

This is what the Effusive Fan said at that moment, and I swear to you, it's the God's honest truth.

EFFUSIVE FAN: Mr. Myers, what do you have coming out?

ME: [*weakly, disbelieving*] . . . *Shrek 2.*

79

That was it. The last straw. If he was going to stay in this tiny bathroom, he would have to pay the price. It was at that moment that a demon inside of me was released into that toilet bowl. A barking demon.

Pee-pee out my bum-bum with such force that I was lifted off the seat, thus proving the Newtonian law of inverse and opposite reaction. Let me put it this way: there was foam in the bowl.

It was bad.

Very bad.

A wafting so bad that it made the door handle hot. It was so bad that it was making the wallpaper curl. It was so bad that even *I* couldn't tolerate it and I questioned its origin, for surely this fetid fog was not of this world. I was in a shame spiral. I don't know how the Effusive Fan was still living. But he was . . .

EFFUSIVE FAN: What else do you have coming out?

I didn't even answer at this point. And by now, I wasn't running the show. Mr. Bowel was in charge, and he was just getting started. The second wave was more staccato. Louder, and significantly more humiliating. It took a while. While I sat there in the crime scene, I was thinking of two things: 1) I had wanted to be a public person my whole life, and here I was, pants around the ankles, in the world's smallest bathroom stall, literally stripped of all dignity. And 2) How fast could I find this funny? I started to laugh, finished up, and left the stall.

EFFUSIVE FAN: [*holding hand out*]
Put it there.

I non-verbally nodded to the carnage behind me and calmly said:

ME: Hey, buddy, let me wash my hands first.

I went to the sink, noticing that the fog had indeed taken the shape of its container, the bathroom. It was bad. Everywhere. I thought to myself, if he didn't have the sense to leave the bathroom, I'm going to take my sweet time washing my hands. And so I pumped the soap container a good fifteen times, partly to further punish, and partly in a vain attempt to freshen the air. I washed my hands thoroughly, to the elbows, like a surgeon. In my head, I ran through the alphabet twice. He stuck his hand out again. I went past him to the hand dryer. Although I would typically give up halfway through the drying time and just wipe my hands on my jeans, on this occasion I stayed for the entire cycle, sarcastically smiling at him as if to say, "Nice in here, huh? Aren't you glad you stayed the whole time?" He was oblivious to my non-verbal communication.

I shook his hand. Although I will spend many incarnations of my soul not understanding how, he told me that I had made his day.

That's what being famous mostly feels like. Hours of shame sprinkled with moments of unexpected and unexplainable validation. But as I listened to my name being said on CHUM by Kori Skinner's dad, in that rent-controlled apartment building in the suburbs of Toronto in the 1960s, everything about celebrity seemed great.

Even Canadian children's television seemed exciting, though in retrospect, it was unbelievably low-budget with very little action. Literally a dude, a three-walled set, and sock puppets. One of the great joys of being Canadian was knowing that our television shows were a little low-rent.

Mr. Dressup was a Canadian children's show that was Canada's answer to *Mister Rogers' Neighborhood*. Unlike *Mister Rogers' Neighborhood*, we never got out of Mr. Dressup's three-walled set that was his house. Mr. Dressup, played by Ernie Coombs, would draw and he would wear costumes that he got from the "tickle trunk." As you might imagine, there is a whole generation of Canadian potheads who refer to the place where they store their weed as the "tickle trunk." Mr. Dressup was joined by two hand puppets: Casey, a young boy, and Finnegan, his dog. Casey, the young Canadian boy, was inexplicably voiced by Judith Lawrence, an Australian lady with an Australian accent.

AS YOU MIGHT IMAGINE, THERE IS A WHOLE GENERATION OF POTHEADS WHO REFER TO THE PLACE WHERE THEY STORE THEIR WEED AS THE "TICKLE TRUNK."

Everything in Canadian children's television was about being cozy, warm, and safe. Even *The Friendly Giant*, a television show about, yes, a friendly giant. He had a one-panel set with a window where he could talk to Jerome the Giraffe and a bag on the wall where he could talk to Rusty the Rooster. Rusty was a bit of a prick. He was argumentative and contrary, whereas Jerome was affable to a fault. I've just reread the last three sentences—I think I have gone insane. No, it happened. I remember watching *The Friendly Giant* with my brothers. At one point the giant always says, "One little chair for one of you, and a bigger chair for two more to curl up in, and for someone who likes to rock, a rocking chair in the middle." When the Friendly Giant said, "for someone who likes to rock," we would break into air guitar. My brothers were and are funny.

Much funnier than I am. Most of my obser-vations of Canadian life exist because I wanted to try to keep up with them. Never under-estimate what a leg up it is in show business to have older brothers who are funny and cool. Thank you, brothers, I love you.

For the most part, cartoons were American. We too had *The Archies*, *Josie and the Pussycats*, and *The Flintstones*. In Quebec, *The Flintstones* is called *Les Pierrafeu*. *Pierrafeu* means, literally, "rock of fire." Fred and Délima Caillou (Fred and Wilma Flintstone) hang out with Arthur and Bertha Laroche (Barney and Betty Rubble). Bam-Bam is Boum-Boum. We thought it was the most hilarious thing in the world.

There was one Canadian cartoon called *Rocket Robin Hood*. It was the Robin Hood story, set in space. It was so low-budget that the characters would repeat the same moves over and over again, and those moves could only happen every five seconds. It was like watching a graphic novel.

Of a higher quality was the live-action CBC show *King of Kensington*. It took place in the culturally diverse

Above, left: Billy Van was a Canadian comedic actor, who, in 1971, was the star of the children's show—produced out of Hamilton, Ontario—called *The Hilarious House of Frightenstein*. It was as if *H.R. Pufnstuf* and *Laugh-in* had a baby. Van played multiple hilarious characters. I used to watch this show after school, and it had a big influence on me. Thank you, Billy.

Above, right: The Friendly Giant rocks.

Kensington Market area of Toronto and starred Al Waxman, of *Cagney and Lacey* fame. The characters were recognizably Torontonian. I thought *King of Kensington* was as close to an American sitcom as Canada ever got. The lighting was fairly good, the sets were lush, the humour was local, and it had great pacing. I felt that Al Waxman and the entire cast really wanted to do well for Canada, and they tried their best to give the Canadian taxpayers, who paid for the CBC, value for their money.

I spent the first eleven years of my life in North York, the suburb next to Scarborough. North York is remarkable for a precipitous style of large rental apartment building known architecturally as the "tower in the park" style, a

mass-produced knockoff of a Le Corbusier "form follows function" design. They were boxy, clad in white brick, usually around seventeen storeys, cheaply built and hastily constructed. Those buildings have the antiseptic charm of a tuberculosis ward. Almost every photograph of me as a kid from that time has one of those tower-in-the-park apartment buildings in the background.

The exterior walls of the apartments were cinder block, topped by a row of windows so poorly insulated that my brothers and I could scrape the frost off the corners of the windows and have snowball fights inside the apartment. Often, during cold winter nights, my brothers and I would open up the window to the bedroom to make ourselves cold. Wearing nothing but our pyjamas, we would see how long we could hold out before we needed to shut the window. Once the window was shut, we dove into our beds to warm up. Once warm, we were soon asleep. I have an abiding love of simple pleasures. And that apartment played a large role in that love.

One of my fondest memories of that apartment is when my brother Paul brought home the newly released Beatles album *Let It Be*. We placed the album on our Canadian-made Clairtone stereo record player, which was mounted in one of those large wooden cabinets that looked almost like a casket but with four legs.

We were never cold, but we were also never warm. It was one of those freezing yet remarkably sunny December days that you get in Toronto. The sun created a hot patch on our rug, and my brothers, our cat, Alexander Mundy, and I sat in that hot patch and listened to that Beatles masterpiece, our minds thoroughly blown. If you had time-lapse photographed that afternoon, you would have watched us lazily move along the carpet, following the warm sun patch.

My brother was able to buy *Let It Be* because all three of us had paper routes. I remember being in that building at five o'clock in the morning, delivering *The Globe and Mail*, and then later that night having to collect payment from the people on my route. I hated and loved "collecting." Some of my customers were nice, and it felt like a performance to knock on the door and say/sing, "Collecting for the *Globe*!" The hard part was when people didn't, or couldn't, pay. Sometimes my dad would get involved, but mostly, I just struck them off my route. To this day, I have the sense memory of how each floor had a unique smell of home cooking. Indian food, Jamaican food, barbecues on the balcony. My brother Peter, ever industrious, had three paper routes. He worked himself so hard that he got a hernia, for which the *Toronto Telegram* gave him an award known as the Golden Bag. The irony is that the hernia had caused him to have a bright blue swollen bag, as blood had collected in his scrotum. You might imagine, to three infantile boys, how fantastically hilarious it was to have an award known as the Golden Bag.

My brothers and I were always looking for ways to make money. Going door to door through our apartment building, collecting pop bottles, was one of them. But sometimes money just came to you, out of nowhere. One time, I was with my mum at a Dominion supermarket. I was wearing a snowsuit, looking at a

bike near the front doors, when a photographer turned to my mum and asked, "Can we take your son's picture and put it in every Dominion store across Canada? We'll pay you." My mum, of course, immediately said yes. This was my first paid gig.

Another way to stretch the budget for working people in Canada was through Canadian Tire money. Canadian Tire, heretofore referred to as Crappy Tire, had a loyalty program wherein, for every purchase, you would be rebated a percentage in the form of scrip, or coupons, you could use toward future purchases. In many ways, my dad valued Canadian Tire money more than the Canadian dollar.

I have an obsession with certain pieces of Canadiana like Canadian Tire money, but nothing matches the obsession I have for the Toronto Transit Commission, Toronto's public transportation service, otherwise known as the TTC, "The Better Way," or, after its red

streetcars, the Red Rocket. The TTC is heavily subsidized by local, provincial, and federal governments, and for a working person, a safe, clean, reliable, comprehensive, and affordable transit system, where the seats aren't ripped up and the floors are immaculate, is a godsend. But to have all of that *and* fantastic signage, logos, and a consistent colour scheme and platform designs is beyond a godsend, especially when you know that this is a government program.

The most remarkable Canadian governmental program that my family and I have ever benefited from was the Ontario Health Insurance Plan (OHIP). OHIP is the provincially run, single-payer health insurance system. Like all families, we've had our share of medical drama, but as a kid I never feared we would be out on the street if one of us got a catastrophic illness. OHIP is not free—our tax rate is slightly higher than some countries. OHIP is not a perfect system, but in a world of nO-HIP, OHIP looks pretty good. OHIP (and all of the other provincial single-payer systems across the nation) is one of the things I am most proud of in Canada.

The public schools that I went to in Canada, in retrospect, were pretty fantastic. Clean, safe, with a high level of achievement expected of you. Whatever *Welcome Back, Kotter* was, Canada wasn't. Not to say it was *Harry Potter*, but it was somewhere in between. For me, I feel that there has been a fantastic return on the money that was paid in taxes for my Canadian public school education. I feel that I was prepared for citizenship and that the playing field was levelled.

In fact, my political philosophy could be called "level playing field–ism." I'm a progressive capitalist.

If you build a better mousetrap, you should be rewarded for that mousetrap. But I also believe that all capable citizens should be given the chance to build that better mousetrap. Talent is a blind pixie that taps its wand on the prodigious, unaware of whether you're male or female, white or a person of colour, gay or straight, rich or poor. Mostly, I believe in the Just Society that my hero, Prime Minister Pierre Elliott Trudeau, described:

> The Just Society will be one in which the rights of minorities will be safe from the whims of intolerant majorities. The Just Society will be one in which those regions and groups which have not fully shared in the country's affluence will be given a better opportunity. The Just Society will be one where such urban problems as housing and pollution will be attacked through the application of new knowledge and new techniques. The Just Society will be one in which our Indian and Inuit populations will be encouraged to assume the full rights of citizenship through policies which will give them both greater responsibility for their own future and more meaningful equality of opportunity. The Just Society will be a united Canada, united because all of its citizens will be actively involved in the development of a country where equality of opportunity is ensured and individuals are permitted to fulfill themselves in the fashion they judge best.

What a fantastic platform, and what a fantastic time in politics that was, when politicians proffered their opinions about governance as opposed to the current trend in politics where politicians proffer their opinions about their opponents. I have benefitted greatly from governmental attempts to level the playing field.

In 1975, we moved from North York to Scarborough into a rent-subsidized government co-op. It was a Canada Mortgage and Housing Corporation (CMHC) townhouse. The CMHC is a government corporation set up to help new Canadian families enter the housing market. Part of your rent was subsidized, part went to the CMHC, and another part went towards the purchase of a house. We went from apartment living to townhouse living. In Scarborough.

In Toronto, Scarborough has the delightful nickname of Scarberia. While there are some rough bits, Scarborough is predominantly working class to middle class, with lovely neighbour-hoods and some upmarket subdivisions. Many of the Scarborough subdivisions made in the seventies have a strange, Soviet, yet petit bourgeois quality. The net effect is that some of these so-called "nice houses" end up looking like a combination of a steak house and a funeral home—a lot of wrought-iron exterior lanterns, partial fieldstone walls, poor man's Gothic. Scarborough is plagued by a crushing flatness, ubiquitous car dealerships, factory carpet outlets, and strip malls.

Scarborough is where I learned the joys of low-level juvenile delinquency, and, more than any other borough of Toronto, Scarborough has produced more of what I

SCARBOROUGH IS WHERE I LEARNED THE JOYS OF LOW-LEVEL JUVENILE DELINQUENCY.

call "juvenile delinquent geniuses." This is not a contradiction in terms. I hung out with a bad group of kids in Scarborough, all of them juvies. But they were good at being juvies.

My juvenile delinquent mentor was a kid we shall call Billy. Billy lived in one of the "nice houses," and his mum was what I believe the kids now refer to as a MILF. A flight attendant for Air Canada, she dressed provocatively, even though she was well past the "best before" date—what my dad would call "mutton dressed as lamb." Billy's dad was a successful businessman who lived in Jupiter, Florida, and was often described by Billy's mum as "a powerful man"; what his "powers" were, exactly, was left to the imagination. Billy's dad would visit once every two months. He would arrive with a "hero gift," usually something like a mini-bike. In the interim, each time I went over to Billy's house, his mum was entertaining a different man, all of whom wore the same shorty robe. Billy called these gentlemen "Mummy's special sleepover friends."

Billy took his delinquency to performance-art levels. One "performance" involved scamming the deposit on milk jugs.

But first, let me take this moment to acknowledge that Canada has a complicated relationship when it comes to the packaging of milk. Milk is packaged in three ways in Canada: the first is the standard card-board carton. The second is . . . *plastic bags*. Milk is sold in plastic bags that are roughly the same size and shape as IV bags and require a specially-made pitcher. One would assume that you would pour the milk into this pitcher, but no . . . one places the unopened milk bag *inside* the pitcher (good luck), and then cuts one

corner of the milk bag to allow pouring. If you cut the corner too much, you get a milk tsunami. Too little, and it's a dribble. There are two words for this design: *inexplicable* and *demented*. Speaking of demented, let's get back to Billy.

Billy's milk jug scam involved the third type of Canadian milk packaging: gallon jugs. At the local Dominion, you could return empty gallon jugs for a ten-cent deposit. The disinterested cashiers at Dominion never looked up when milk jugs were being returned to the bin in front of their cash register. When they heard the rattle of the jugs, without looking, they would robotically ask, "How many?"

Here's where Billy's genius came into play. He would simply shake the deposit bin, offering no milk jugs. The

unsuspecting cashier would ask, "How many?" Billy would coolly reply, "Ten." He used the ill-gotten dollar to pay for the candy that he was buying—as a cover for the stolen candy stuffed in his bomber jacket. He would steal Hostess Hickory Sticks, Tahiti Treat soda, Big Turk chocolate bars, Eat-Mores, Mr. Big, and Lik-M-Aid. One day, he shoplifted a turkey. Another day, shrimp salad. Unsatisfied with the plain shrimp, he went back in and

shoplifted cocktail sauce. Then he went home and stole a bottle of cheap wine you could only get in Canada, depressingly named Lonesome Charlie. Lonesome Charlie's tagline was, "Lonesome Charlie is looking for a friend." (Wow . . . morbid *and* bleak.)

The most surreal example of Billy's juvenile delinquent genius was the Manhole Cover Incident. We had been throwing snowballs at cars, and we'd been bumper hitching. For those of you not familiar with bumper hitching, it was the insanely unsafe, and I hope illegal, practice of grabbing on to the bumper of a car driving on a snowy street. We called it "Scarborough water skiing." Volkswagen Beetles were the best to bumper hitch, because the tubing on the rear bumper formed unintended handles. The best results for bumper hitching were achieved by wearing hard shoes with no tread, like Peter Pan getaway boots.

Billy noticed that some workers from Bell Canada had gone to lunch and left their gear by the side of the road. He picked up a manhole cover crowbar, opened up a manhole in the middle of the road, and wedged the crowbar so that it was sticking straight up.

I watched in disbelieving silence. I didn't know where this was going. Then a car came along and smashed its front end into the crowbar. Billy started laughing uncontrollably. The driver came out pissed. Billy then started to shout toward the manhole cover, "Jim! Run! He's coming down into the manhole to get you!" Billy lied that there was a kid in the sewer who was sticking the crowbar out of the manhole to damage passing cars. Of course, there was no Jim, and the driver removed the manhole cover and went down into the manhole, chasing after "Jim."

As soon as the driver was at the bottom of the ladder, Billy calmly slid the manhole cover back into place, got into the driver's car, and rolled the car so that the front wheel was on top of the manhole cover, trapping the driver down inside the manhole. Then Billy shouted down at him, "You asshole!" as if it was the driver's fault.

I'm not going to sit here and say that it was right. But it takes the mind of a genius to move juvenile delinquency to the next dimension: performance art.

During the winter months, we would have endless table hockey tournaments. One day, in mid-tournament, Billy turned to us and asked if we were hungry. We were too busy, so he excused himself, saying he was going upstairs to make a meal. Twenty minutes later, he came downstairs with a Chinet plate with what appeared to be sausages and some sort of vegetable. But as soon as he came down, there was a horrible stench.

Of course, if you get eight young boys together, someone will inevitably fart, but this was . . . different. And Billy seemed oblivious. Unnoticed was the fact that Billy was now wearing nice clothes, had combed his hair with an old-timey middle part, had a napkin tucked into his shirt mob-style, and was incessantly fussing with his cutlery, never really digging into his sausage.

Upon further examination of the sausage, it was clear that he had, in fact, taken a dump on the Chinet plate and garnished his turd sausages with parsley! I had to choose between laughing and throwing up in my mouth. I chose laughing. I don't know how he thought such a thing up. And while genius is usually reserved for accomplishments like string theory, part of me thinks that Billy might actually be juvenile delinquency's first bona fide genius.

When I tell people about my life in Scarborough the first question they ask is, "Where were the parents?" Billy's home life was dreadful. He was often scolded and humiliated by his mum. His dad was a no-show. And then, of course, there were "Mummy's special sleepover friends." He was left unattended most of the time, which for us meant that his basement was our playhouse. This period of time, my unattended juvenile delinquent years in Scarborough, is the basis of everything that I wanted to include in the *Wayne's World* movies. Where were their parents?

I love hockey. But as I mentioned earlier, I didn't play ice hockey seriously until I was thirty. My Scarborough years were all about street hockey, floor hockey, table hockey, and watching *Hockey Night in Canada*. From my earliest memory, I have loved the Toronto Maple Leafs. I love the name. I love that we wear blue. I love the maple leaf. I love the grammatical idiosyncrasy of the name of the team. I love the little maple leaf on the shoulders of the team sweater. And I love the three broad stripes, surrounded by two narrow stripes, on our hockey socks. I love how a Maple Leafs player looks on a table hockey table, on a hockey card, on a Power Players stamp. I love the look of

I LOVE THE MAPLE LEAFS. I LOVE THE GRAMMATICAL IDIOSYNCRASY OF THE NAME.

Maple Leaf Gardens, the art deco masterpiece. I love the Gardens marquee and I loved Doug Laurie Sports, the souvenir and sporting goods shop inside. I loved *Hockey Night in Canada*'s gondola—the broadcast booth precariously suspended from the ceiling of the Gardens. I loved the *Hockey Night in Canada* theme. I think the *HNIC* theme could be a good backup for "O Canada." I loved the old *Hockey Night in Canada* logo, the side stick one. I always wanted to get a powder blue *HNIC* blazer with the side stick logo embroidered on the pocket. I love Don Cherry. "Coach's Corner" is a mainline hit of Canadiana and Ron MacLean's Canadian accent is so thick that even I have a hard time understanding it sometimes. I loved Danny Gallivan and his "cannonading drives," "scintillating saves," and "Savardian spin-o-ramas."

And then, of course, there were fantastic moments, like the time *HNIC* experimented with putting a camera and microphone on the players' bench—forgetting, of course, that hockey players take trash talk to a cruel and offensive extreme. The first time they cut to the bench in a game, a young, toothless Bobby Clarke admonished referee Bruce Hood, saying, "Why don't you go fuck yourself, Hood, you fuckin' queer." That experiment was quickly abandoned. No more bench cam.

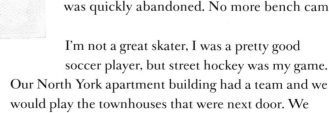

I'm not a great skater, I was a pretty good soccer player, but street hockey was my game. Our North York apartment building had a team and we would play the townhouses that were next door. We played in their rundown tennis court, which, for us, was

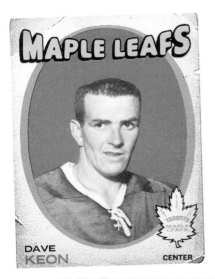

MAPLE LEAFS

DAVE
KEON   CENTER

HOCKEY
CHECKLIST

1	Poul Popiel	30	Norm Ullman
2	Pierre Bouchard	31	T. Williams
3	Don Awrey	32	Ted Harris
4	Paul Curtis	33	Andre Lacroix
5	Guy Trottier	34	Mike Byers
6	Paul Shmyr	35	Johnny Bucyk
7	Fred Stanfield	36	Roger Crozier
8	Mike Robitaille	37	A. Delvecchio
9	Vic Hadfield	38	F. St. Marseille
10	Jim Harrison	39	Pit Martin
11	Bill White	40	Brad Park
12	Andre Boudrias	41	Greg Polis
13	Gary Sabourin	42	O. Kurtenbach
14	Arnie Brown	43	Jim McKenny
15	Yvan Cournoyer	44	Bob Nevin
16	Bryan Hextall	45	Ken Dryden
17	Gary Croteau	46	Carol Vadnais
18	Gilles Villemure	47	Bill Flett
19	Serge Bernier	48	Jim Johnson
20	Phil Esposito	49	Allan Hamilton
21	Tom Reid	50	Bobby Hull
22	Doug Barrie	51	C. Bordeleau
23	Eddie Joyal	52	Tim Ecclestone
24	Dunc. Wilson	53	Rod Seiling
25	Pat Stapleton	54	G. Cheevers
26	Garry Unger	55	B. Goldsworthy
27	Al Smith	56	Ron Schock
28	Bob Woytowich	57	Jim Dorey
29	Marc Tardiff	58	Wayne Maki

a rink of dreams. You could shoot on net and if you missed, you didn't have to run 100 yards to retrieve the ball. The watertight surface meant that if everyone slapshotted away the puddles after it rained, we could be up and running within fifteen minutes. Our goalie pads were made of stolen or found sofa cushions. A baseball glove was the goalie glove. And a blocker was made out of an egg carton duct-taped to a hockey glove. If you pretended to be hurt, you were a "faker"; the only thing worse than being a faker was being a "hacker." A hacker was somebody who hacked at your stick incessantly. If you hung out by the other team's goal and never came back to play defence, you were a "goal suck," and only a dink would take a slapshot from two feet out. Our biggest fear was being "squared," which was getting hit in the nuts. (Why does getting hit in the nuts give you a stomach ache?) The worst thing was to overcelebrate your goal, because then you would be considered "conceited."

We didn't have a lot of money for hockey gear. I remember the day when I went from Hespeler hockey sticks bought at Canadian Tire to plastic Mylec blades that you would curve at home, over the stove. Every one of my Mylec blades ended up with concentric-circle stove burns. At school, it was a day to be celebrated when gym class let you play floor hockey with the plastic sticks and hollow plastic pucks. If you could raise a hollow plastic puck, you were a god. I was a floor-hockey god.

At recess, we traded hockey cards. One guy would shuffle through his stack, showing you what he had, to which you would say, "Got 'im. Got 'im. Need 'im. Need 'im. Got 'im. Got 'im. Checklist." Checklist was an informational card that just listed all of the players that made a complete set. I once traded a Davey Keon for a checklist, using my brother Peter's stack by accident. "You traded my Keon for checklist?" To which I replied, "Checklist is a card! And I have four Keons!" In reality, the checklist was *not* a card. I had failed. At the end of the season, after someone had laboriously completed a full set, the hockey cards would be thrown in the air. Kindergarten kids would frantically pick them up, cracking heads as they did so.

By June, if you're a Leafs fan, the season is over. Truthfully, it's usually over by December. Every year, the Leafs have a great team on paper, but unfortunately, hockey is played on ice. Similarly, every

September, the Toronto press have the Leafs winning the Stanley Cup, but alas, the Stanley Cup final is not until June. By that time, my thoughts would have turned away from hockey and toward the summer, which meant the Canadian National Exhibition—the CNE, or, even shorter, the Ex.

All year long, I'd save up my "Ex money," and this could be supplemented by "Ex dollars," which were promotional scrip printed in the *Toronto Telegram*. By going to the garbage-chute room and rifling through discarded *Telegram*s, my brothers and I could cut out an extra fifty dollars each. In reality, only ten Ex dollars were ever honoured. Most places at the Ex wanted real money.

The CNE was an old fair. Even by the seventies, it looked like it needed a lick of paint. It seemed permanent, but somehow temporary, like a downmarket Disney World representation of the British Empire. But to me it was . . . exotic, worldly. I felt like James Joyce's character in the short story "Araby" from his *Dubliners* collection. In the story, Araby was the name of the rundown, Arabia-themed bazaar in the heart of the otherwise dull and drab Dublin. It was a magic zone where anything could happen.

You entered the CNE through the majestic Beaux Arts masterpiece known as the Princes' Gate, or as kids in Scarborough call it, the Princess Gate. This gate was, in many ways, more ornate and impressive than the Brandenburg Gate in Berlin. Once past the gate, your free-admission ticket that came with your report card accepted, you were in the heart of the Midway. The Midway was the main street that had all the rides. The Flyer was the premier roller coaster: wooden, rickety, a fire trap. I rode it; I survived it. Another roller coaster, the Wildcat, was a cool, modern, tubular roller coaster and was okay but not worth the long line. The Wild Mouse, on the other hand, was narrow-gauged, dubiously constructed, with corners and dropoffs that defied physics. Rumour had it that twenty children in Europe had been killed on the Wild Mouse (morbid). So, the Wild Mouse needed to be tamed. I passed this *rite de passage* with flying colours.

Blaring from the speakers of the Bobsled ride was a police siren and warning bells, augmented by a deafening disc jockey, who kept saying, "Do you want to go fastah?" The Bobsled itself was fast but disappointing because it only went around in a circle, backwards. I'm not certain how that made it a bobsled, and the only thing I remember was the annoying disc jockey repeatedly saying, "Do you want to go fastah?" Even today, if I say, "Do you want to go fastah?" any Torontonian immediately will say, "The Bobsled." That's one of two catchphrases that the CNE had. The

other catchphrase came from a guy who sold trick animal leashes, which he claimed were invisible dogs. All day long, with the aid of a heavily distorted microphone, he singsonged the same two words: "Doggie *daahh*-gie." By the time you went home, you were convinced your name was Doggie Doggie.

My strongest recollection, which I'm sure is wrong, is that the Midway blasted "Lady Marmalade" by Labelle on an endless loop. And because my brothers and I took French in school, we knew the raunchy-sounding chorus went "Do you want to go to bed with me . . . tonight?" It was awesome. Less clear, however, was the English translation of "Gitchie, gitchie, ya ya dada."

The sideshows on the Midway were remarkably shoddy. Years of apathy had taken their toll on the quality of the haunted houses. They weren't scary; they were sad. One haunted house on a tractor trailer had a "scary greeter," which, through years of neglect, was now just a guy with long, greasy hair, a denim jacket, sloppily applied KISS makeup, smoking a butt, reading the *Toronto Sun*. As you passed him, without looking up from the hockey page, he would blow out a puff of smoke and give you a perfunctory, monotone "Boo." I demand more of my haunted houses.

Next to the Midway, in the more permanent buildings, were trade shows. There was the Better Living Centre, where I first saw a push-button phone, and the old British art deco–styled Automotive Building, which we called the "Avtomotive Bvilding," not realizing that the *V*s were actually *U*s from the classical carving style. Inside the Automotive Building, car makers would give you free promotional mini-cars. We, of course, lamented that there were no Canadian cars. We were, however, heartened to see a Canadian Armed Forces pavilion, a Canadian Dairy kiosk (free ice cream!), the Hockey Hall of Fame, where the Stanley Cup permanently lived, and various trade displays, including one from Communist China, which both frightened and fascinated me.

My father sold the *Encyclopaedia Britannica* at the CNE. I loved visiting him. I was so proud of how funny he was with the customers. Selling was his milieu. But the real action was at the Food Building, where Canadian food products were sold at promotional prices. You could get a big box of Double Bubble gum for twenty-five cents. A giant jar of honey was forty cents. Pepsi was a nickel. My tradition was to get a back bacon on a bun from Schneiders. Back bacon is what Americans call Canadian bacon. It has a peameal coating, which is just cornmeal that soaks up all the bacony flavour during frying. I would put a dash of HP Sauce on it, which would be soaked up by the lightly toasted kaiser roll. Heaven.

One year, I had budgeted my money perfectly. I had
left just enough for my back bacon on a bun. But when
I got to the counter, the price had gone up by forty
cents. The twenty-year-old dude working the concession stand read my face perfectly. He said, "Hey, kid, I
get one of these a day. Here, take it." I couldn't believe
the generosity. It shaped my worldview at the time, and
was part of my coming of age. With the extra money, I
got a milkshake from the Neilson Dairy stand, went to
the War of 1812 cannons on the lakeshore, and savoured
every morsel.

Another year, when I was super-young, I saw Mel
Profit, an offensive end for the Toronto Argonauts of
the Canadian Football League. The Argos used to play
at the CNE Stadium. I loved the old double-blue Argos
uniform with the simple *A* on the helmet. I was nervous

to approach Mel because he was a giant and he was the first celebrity I had ever met, but he was nice to me, even though I was a little kid, and even though nobody was looking.

THE MAIN ATTRACTION AT THE CNE WAS ALL THE OLDER TEENAGE GIRLS FROM AROUND TORONTO.

But the main attraction at the CNE was all the older teenage girls from around Toronto. They came from exotic locales with names like Mimico, Etobicoke, Mississauga, Thornhill, East York, Hogg's Hollow, Forest Hill, Humber Valley, Pickering, New Toronto, Don Mills, York Mills, Flemingdon Park, and Moss Park. These Midway beauties were all identical. They all had Farrah Fawcett hair, blue eyeshadow, feather earrings, super-tight GWG jeans, halter tops, and were replete with the fragrance of Tickle deodorant and Dr. Pepper chapstick. They all seemed like movie stars to me.

By the time I was old enough to go to the CNE with an actual real-life girl, I rarely ran out of money, because I had continued to do Canadian television commercials. One of the commercials I did was for Wrigley's Spearmint gum. Even though it was for the Canadian market, it was shot in Los Angeles, days before Christmas; I remember seeing Santa decorations affixed to palm trees. The commercial is set in an overnight camp. There's a camp counsellor, and I play one of the campers. The unfortunate part was that the dialogue went as follows:

CAMP COUNSELLOR: Hey, Joey.

ME: Hey, Jack. Want some gum?

CAMP COUNSELLOR: Candy flavoured?

ME: No, it's Wrigley's.

CAMP COUNSELLOR: Oh, you graduated to the Big Stick.

Left: Alas, the Boo-jee hat.

Now, the big stick in question, of course, is Wrigley's gum. But when you're twelve years old in Scarborough, your friends see the "Big Stick" a little differently. Word got out that I was Joey from the TV commercial. Kids I'd never met at school would come up to me and say, "Hey, are you Joey?" Reluctantly, I'd say, "Yes . . ." "I hear you've graduated to the Big Stick! Fuck you, faggot!"

It was tough. There were fights. I won many of them. The low point was during final exams. Three different kids interrupted the quiet exam room by shouting into the classroom, "Which one's Joey?" My classmates gave me up immediately. "Nice Big Stick, faggot." It was my first catchphrase, and it would not be my last.

In fact, everything I did, even as a child, ended up being a catchphrase at school. When I had a guest spot on *The Littlest Hobo*, a show about a stray dog that goes from town to town, I had the line, "Wow, that dog's a real Frisbee hound." Unfortunately, my thick Canadian accent made it sound like "Frisbee hoond." So I was treated to "That dog's a real Frisbee hoond." Then I was the host of a disco show on local TV called *Boogie Jr.*, which my English mother insisted on calling "Boo-jee

107

Jr." I was a heavy metal kid. I loved Zeppelin, Rush, and a local band called Max Webster. I was miserable hosting a disco show. At one point, the producer encouraged me to loosen up, and so I introduced the song "Dance the Kung Fu" while waving my arms around doing "kung fu" moves. As a result, the microphone only picked up every second word, and my intro ended up sounding like "Ants ung oo." From that point on, if I ever got too full of myself, my brothers would put me in my place by saying, "Ants ung oo." Or if they *really* wanted to tear me down, they would set me up with things like, "That's really smart, Mike. Did you learn that from that Chinese philosopher?" And I would say, "What Chinese philosopher?" And they'd say, "You know, the Chinese philosopher Ants Ung Oo?" Ego death.

In 1975, I was on *King of Kensington* playing a Canadian Boy Scout con man who rips Al Waxman off. The catchphrase from that show was me telling Al Waxman, "Shove off, fat boy."

By the time I started high school I had lost interest in show business. It had less to do with the taunting and more to do with the fact that I had gone to England by myself in the summer of 1977, the year punk rock broke in London. My cousins north of London had taken me to a punk club, gotten me drunk, and had purchased for me the Sex Pistols single "God Save the Queen." I was hooked. It was raw, quirky, fun, and funny.

The only problem was that my dad, a staunch monarchist, would never let a record featuring the lyrics "God save the Queen, she ain't no human being" into his proper English house. I ended up putting the Sex Pistols single into a Jimi Hendrix sleeve. Little did I know, my father was a giant Hendrix fan, likening Jimi's guitar prowess to Django Reinhardt. The Sex Pistols single was immediately found and confiscated, but my love of punk was unabated.

My first high school, Sir John A. Macdonald Collegiate Institute, was in Scarborough, and was named after Canada's first prime minister. It was a heavy metal school—very macho, lots of long hair, people wearing flared jeans. Like many suburban schools, conformity was king. As a punk rocker with short, spiky hair, a leather jacket, and ripped, tapered black jeans, I stuck out. My social life was not in the suburbs, it was downtown, where there were other punks, cool record stores, and Toronto's fantastic second-run cinema

Me in the insanely low-budget CBC children's television special *Range Ryder and the Calgary Kid*. I played the Calgary Kid. If you take the time to YouTube this, check out the dinosaurs. Low budge!

scene, which comprised between eight and ten amazing old theatres that projected themed double features, like *The Seventh Seal* and *The Seven Samurai*, or *400 Blows* and Jean-Luc Godard's *Breathless*.

My best friend Dave Mackenzie's classmate at Macdonald was a guy named David Furnish. I remember seeing David Furnish in the halls, and I thought he was a nice dude, but he was a year younger than me, and sometimes in high school that creates a weird separation. Many years later I would meet that same David Furnish again. I was at my first Hollywood party, right after finishing the movie *Wayne's World*. It was Elton John's Oscar party, and I had never seen so many famous people in one room: Oliver Stone, Sean Connery, Rob Lowe, Sharon Stone, Demi Moore, Sylvester Stallone—it was weird. Elton John shouted in my direction, "You! I've been waiting for you!"

As a joke, I turned to my friends and said, "Yeah, Elton's been expecting me."

Then Elton said, "Mike Myers! There's someone I want you to meet."

I didn't know anybody at this party, but there was one guy who looked like David Furnish. And then David, in his Canadian accent, said, "Hey, Mike. It's me, David Furnish, Davey Mackenzie's friend."

I went, "Holy shit, are *we* out of context."

And then David Furnish said, "We're a long way from Scarborough, eh, buddy?"

I said, "Indeed."

He said, "Isn't it weird? You're a movie star, and I'm Elton John's wife, eh?"

I said, "It's all weird, buddy."

He said, "Betcha didn't know I was gay, eh?"

> HE SAID, "ISN'T IT WEIRD? YOU'RE A MOVIE STAR, AND I'M ELTON JOHN'S WIFE, EH?"

My brother Paul is a great artist. In high school he was obsessed with Polaroids, especially the thick bottom part that he called the "icon." Note the use of Letraset on the icon.

paul
myers
'81

MOTION
PICTURE
#1

On a side note, Elton is a sports fan, having once owned the English soccer team Watford FC. At that party, he and I had the most in-depth conversation about what the Leafs needed to do to turn the organization around. With encyclopedic knowledge, he went player by player through the Leafs roster. By some stroke of good luck, I had spent the day reading my *Hockey News*.

While at Sir John A. Macdonald Collegiate, I heard about another high school in the suburbs of Scarborough named Stephen Leacock Collegiate Institute. Leacock had a million-dollar television studio on campus. I wanted to be a movie director so I transferred to Leacock and took the TV course, which was fantastic.

On the weekends, I went downtown and was the opening comedy act for punk bands at various clubs around the city. On that scene was a punk band called L'Étranger that was getting a nice following. They were very political in that Clash way. Two members of L'Étranger, Andrew Cash and Chuck Angus, also went

to Leacock. I remember talking politics with them and bonding with them over the duality of our suburban school weeks and downtown punk weekends. Both went on to become members of the Canadian Parliament.

I started to try to include the suburban/downtown duality in my act. I created a character based on all of my suburban heavy metal friends from Scarborough. I tried to think of the most Canadian name possible, and I came up with Wayne Campbell.

One of the great bands in the Toronto punk scene, Drastic Measures, let me open for them as Wayne Campbell on several occasions. Their lead singer, Tony Malone, was hilarious in his own right, and a brilliant songwriter. He was a source of tremendous encouragement to me. Thank you, Tony.

Also roaming the halls of Leacock was an aspiring young actor named Eric McCormack. He was in the theatre clique, which I knew tangentially. But I was more into comedy than drama. Of course, McCormack, a brilliant comedic actor, would go on to star in the hit television show *Will & Grace*. Ironically, Eric later went to Macdonald and became friends himself with David Furnish. It's a small world, but when all three of us Scarborough boys bumped into each other many years later at the Cannes Film Festival, it felt tiny.

By now, I had started to take the Second City theatre workshop program. It's from this program that people were hired for the Second City touring company—the junior company of the Second City mainstage company that performed eight shows a week, six nights a week, at the landmark Old Firehall. The workshops were awesome: challenging, educational, and I ended up making the acquaintance of the brilliant Dave

Foley, who was taking workshops and beginning to form the Kids in the Hall. It was an exciting time of music, comedy, and movies. I went to the movies three times a week, took workshops twice a week, and met Dave Foley for coffee, learning everything I could from the man I consider the smartest person I've ever met.

Meanwhile, at school the government required that you take an aptitude test. It was twenty pages long, and the results of your test were sent to Ottawa, Canada's capital, for assessment by a government employee, who would tell you what they thought you should do for a living. For shits and giggles, I decided to answer all the questions as truthfully as possible. I was curious to find out what career Ottawa thought I should pursue. I suspected it would be either architecture or photography.

My results came in: the Canadian government thought I was best suited to be a movie star. Not an actor, not a comedian. A movie star.

I had applied to York University in Toronto, for a fine arts degree in film, to study to become a director. I was also invited to audition for the Second City touring company—if hired, I would become a full-time actor. Ironically, my audition was scheduled for my last day of high school. That morning, I woke to find a letter of acceptance from York University. At 9 a.m., I had my last exam of high school. At noon, I had my audition for the Second City touring company. And at 3 p.m., I was hired for Second City.

It was 1982, and I was still living at home in Scarborough. I ended up not going to York University.

I was a professional actor.

I was an adult, now.

I was nineteen.

I knew what I was doing next with my life, but I was wondering what Canada was going to do next. When we were kids in Scarborough, during the sixties and seventies, we were told that Canada was going to be "The Next Great Nation." I've decided to call this time in Canadian history, between 1967–1976, "The Next Great Nation" era. During this time the Canadian government undertook a massive, nationwide initiative to answer the fundamental Canadian questions, "Who are we?" and "Why are we?" It was a bold attempt, but what was it exactly? And did it work?

PART TWO

Patriot

CHAPTER THREE

"The Next Great Nation"

W HILE IT WAS CLEARLY
America's century, there was a brief time between 1967
and 1976 when Canadians faced their identity malaise
head on. We sought to define ourselves by achieving
greatness: greatness in the arts, in architecture, in
urban design, and progressivism.

It was during this brief nine-year period that the
Canadian government enacted far-reaching policies to
individuate ourselves from Mother Europe and Brother
America in the hopes of defining our identity and in
that definition, perhaps, a mission statement. In 1967,
I was four years old. In 1976, I was thirteen. These were
my formative years, and the Next Great Nation era was
Canada's formative years.

Remarkably, at around the same time (1966), in Red
China, Chairman Mao Zedong had also undertaken an

117

ambitious governmental effort to redefine his country's identity—the Cultural Revolution, in which several million Chinese people were killed. Canada's cultural evolution was much less violent, resulting only in half a dozen terrible television shows. Sure, they were terrible, but they were *our* terrible television shows. For Americans, such big-government spending on culture is unthinkable, and, because of their clear mission statement, it's unnecessary.

THE BRITISH NORTH AMERICA ACT OFFERS CANADIANS "PEACE, ORDER, AND GOOD GOVERNMENT."

The Declaration of Independence clearly guarantees Americans "life, liberty, and the pursuit of happiness." The British North America Act offers Canadians "peace, order, and good government." Not as sexy, and hardly a guarantee, but we do have a history of peace and order. Is this a good thing? I'm reminded of the speech that Orson Welles improvised for his character Harry Lime in the 1949 film *The Third Man*:

> HARRY LIME: . . . In Italy for thirty years under the Borgias they had warfare, terror, murder, and bloodshed, but they produced Michelangelo, Leonardo da Vinci, and the Renaissance. In Switzerland they had brotherly love—they had five hundred years of democracy and peace, and what did that produce? The cuckoo clock.

Has Canada been relegated to "cuckoo clock" status? Can one legislate one's way to an identity? Have civility and big government stunted our cultural growth?

Well, from 1967 to 1976, Canada was going to find out, because unlike our neighbours to the south,

Canada has never had a fear of big government. One example is the Canadian Broadcasting Corporation (CBC), which was created and paid for by the Canadian government in 1936. In 1967, the CBC began creating TV programs by and for Canadians.

The CBC is an enigma wrapped in a bureaucracy. However frustrating we who toil in the fields of comedy find the Ceeb, it does fulfill its mandate and has created a situation whereby Canadians interested in the television industry, and all of its related occupations, can learn. The great Canadian author Malcom Gladwell,

in his book *Outliers*, makes the observation that it takes ten thousand hours of practice to master any given art form. For example, the Beatles became the Beatles by spending ten thousand hours in Hamburg, Germany, free from the scrutiny of British society. When they returned to Liverpool, they were ready to become the "four lads who shook the world."

The CBC allows Canadians to master their craft before shaking the world. Case in point is the CBC show *Dr. Zonk and the Zunkins* (1974), which featured an as-yet-unknown Gilda Radner and soon-to-be-discovered John Candy. Then, a year later, another show, *Coming Up Rosie* (1975), starred the great Canadians Dan Aykroyd and Catherine O'Hara, both of whom were not yet famous. In the show, Dan Aykroyd played a character named Purvis Bickle, who was a Scottish superintendent. I loved this character. Purvis Bickle made me want to do Scottish characters. Dan Aykroyd is a brilliant character comedian whose attention to detail is next to none. One of my favourite Dan Aykroyd characters is Fred Garvin, Male Prostitute. Again, as a Canadian, I recognized his accent to be that of the Ottawa Valley. In my head, the Ottawa Valley accent *is* the Canadian accent. I worship him.

TV shows in Canada don't pay in money, they pay in ten thousand hours of practice. And while there isn't gold in them thar hills, there is the consolation that creative work done in Canada doesn't count against your career.

A list of Canadian actors, filmmakers, and producers who have benefited directly or indirectly from the CBC and all the other government-funded arts programs reads as follows: Wayne and Shuster, Mort Sahl, Lorne Greene, James Cameron, Norman Jewison, Dan Aykroyd, Ryan Gosling, Tommy Chong, David Steinberg, Rich Little, Rick Moranis, Dave Thomas, Martin Short, Eugene Levy, William Shatner (that's right—Kirk is Canadian), Michael J. Fox, Howie Mandel, my dear friends Phil Hartman and Dave Foley, Bruce McCulloch, Kevin McDonald, Mark McKinney, Scott Thompson, Nia Vardalos, Ellen Page, Leslie Nielsen, Jim Carrey, Tom Green, Colin Mochrie, Norm Macdonald, Ryan Reynolds, Seth Rogen, Will Arnett, Michael Cera, and, last but not least, Mr. Lorne Michaels. I'm humbled to be part of this list and I feel like I have the great privilege to do what I do because of big government. That's some list. That's some cuckoo clock.

The governmental programs of the Next Great Nation era inspired all levels of Canadian society. We wanted to take our seat at the world table. In 1967, Canada turned 100. A wave of patriotism spread throughout the nation. It was an exciting time to be Canadian.

One of the peaks of that excitement was that Montreal hosted the 1967 world's fair, known as Expo 67. Its motto was "Man and His World"—Canada had gone global. Each country had its own pavilion. America sported one of the world's first Buckminster Fuller geodesic domes, an engineering marvel that still delights the eye and the intellect. Canada's pavilion looked like an inverted pyramid. To this day, I try to understand the significance of that shape. I'm guessing the inverted pyramid is meant to represent some sort of elevation of the working class. My family and I gave the Canadian pavilion the nickname The Candy Dish.

"MICHAEL'S GONE INTO THE SOVIET PAVILION. I THINK HE'S GOING TO DEFECT!"

Much to my family's terror, at the age of four, I got lost in the U.S.S.R. pavilion, to which my brother Paul exclaimed, "Michael's gone into the Soviet pavilion. I think he's going to defect!" While it's true that Soviet defection was something I had been threatening to do, even as early as two years old, alas, my loyalties were, and continue to be, to the West. As I've said since Grade 1, "Big government is one thing, but a proletarian dictatorship is beyond the pale." My family collected every possible souvenir connected to Expo 67. I still keep an Expo 67 coin in my wallet. I love Montreal and I love that it's part of Canada.

That same year, 1967, Montreal gave Canada another gift. A young minister of justice, under Prime Minister Lester Pearson, announced that Canada was legalizing divorce, abortion, and homosexuality. When asked by the press, "Under what mandate can you propose

L'Exposition universelle
de 1967—
Le Spectacle du Siècle

The 1967
World Exhibition—
Show of the Century

expo67

28 AVRIL–27 OCTOBRE   APRIL 28–OCTOBER 27

MONTRÉAL CANADA

such sweeping changes in Canadian social policy?" the young minister of justice responded confidently, "There's no place for the state in the bedrooms of the nation."

That minister of justice, Pierre Elliott Trudeau, was elected prime minister of Canada in the following year, 1968, and Canada was forever changed. As Kennedy was to America, Trudeau was to Canada, and in several ways, even more so. Due to the dynamic nature of our parliamentary system of government, Trudeau was able to enact much more progressive legislation immediately and without opposition.

In 1968, Trudeau's government passed the Canadian content laws that required a certain percentage of media content seen or heard by Canadians to be at least partially created or produced by Canadians. It came to be known as CanCon. Literally, the government, in the name of creating a Canadian identity, would mandate what could or could not be seen or heard on television or radio. From an American standpoint, this is no different than Mao's Cultural Revolution. But the vast majority of Canadians, swept up in "Trudeaumania," felt a sense of urgency to begin to create a distinct cultural identity. It didn't feel like tyranny, it felt like empowerment. Perhaps in Pierre Trudeau, Canada now had its long-awaited dramaturge.

CanCon dictated that radio stations had to play a percentage of "Canadian" music. CanCon supplied the definition of "Canadian" under the MAPL system. MAPL is an acronym of Music, Artist, Performance, and Lyrics. It meant that in order to qualify as Canadian content, music must have at least two of the following:

M: the music is written by a Canadian

A: the music is, or the lyrics are, performed by a
Canadian artist

P: the musical selection consists of a performance
that is:

- recorded in Canada, or
- performed in Canada and broadcast live
in Canada

L: the lyrics are written by a Canadian

By now, freedom-loving Americans reading this have already put one of their many guns in their mouth, both because of the intention of a law by which a government would mandate culture, and certainly by the byzantine wording of that law. For Canadians, we felt a thrill that our collective voice could be heard over the din of our noisy neighbours to the south.

Even private companies got into the act. In the 1960s and '70s, Sam the Record Man was a massive record store in Toronto. At the height of Sam the Record Man's popularity, there were 130 stores across Canada. The flagship store in Toronto featured a pair of three-storey signs in the shape of vinyl records with sequenced neon lights that gave the illusion that these giant records were spinning. That alone, to a seven-year old, was enough. It felt like show business. It was exciting. There was a Canadian section in the store, and I often would buy albums sight unheard just to give them a chance because they were Canadian. One of those bands was the Stampeders, who ended up having a hit with the song "Sweet City Woman" (1973), which reached number 1 on the Canadian charts and number 8 on the U.S. charts. I even got into jazz by way of Sam the Record Man's Canadian section.

One day, I bought an album by the Canadian jazz pianist Oscar Peterson. I didn't know anything about jazz, but Oscar Peterson was Canadian, so I bought it, and, by the way, loved it, even though at the time I was exclusively into rock.

The Sam in Sam the Record Man was Sam Sniderman. A Canadian hero who simply asked the question, "Why not from Canada?" And this question was spreading like wildfire in Canada. Even to the point of product promotions.

The Canadian subsidiary of the 7Up company had a promotion called Rock Caps. At the bottom of every specially marked can of 7Up, there was the name and face of a Canadian rock band member. The bands were Lighthouse, the Guess Who, April Wine, Crowbar, and Edward Bear. My brothers, Peter and Paul, and I were obsessed. We found ourselves rummaging through the garbage, looking for 7Up cans. Our hands were bloodied because of how hard it is to cut open the bottom of a pop can. We ran the risk of tetanus and other opportunistic infections, but in the end, we got Don DiNovo, the violinist of the rock band Lighthouse, and our collection was complete. We were looking inward, claiming and naming Canadian bands. Joni and Neil were already in the States planting the flag, but now it felt like their U.S. residency was less of an exile and more of a beachhead for these new Canadian recording artists.

Similarly, Shell gas stations in Canada offered commemorative medallions featuring the prime ministers of Canada. The goal was to collect all (at that time) fifteen prime ministers. My favourite prime minister was Charles Tupper. The only thing I knew about Tupper was that he had giant Brooklyn-style mutton chops.

Play 7•UP Rock Caps.

You can win* "Guess Who" London, England concert trips for two,
Datsun 240Z's, Electrohome stereos, rock record albums or posters.

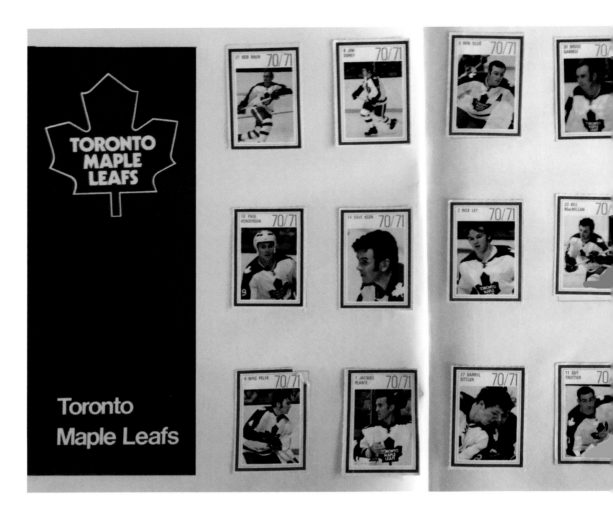

Toronto Maple Leafs

Neil Young. A fine Tupper.

To this day, if my brother Paul and I see a guy with mutton chops we will say, "He's sporting a fine Tupper."

Previous to 1967, the only time you learned about Canadian history was in a classroom. We were attempting to do what Americans do, sewing history into culture.

In 1970, Esso Canada created a hockey card promotion called Esso Power Players. Whenever you filled up your tank, you received a packet of Power Player hockey stickers to fill a Power Player album. Power Players were

a phenomenon. I was addicted. And while some of the NHL players were American, and I think there was one European (a Finn named Juha Widing), the vast majority of the players were from Canada. These were Canadian heroes, and you could only get these stickers in Canada. Americans had baseball cards; we had Power Players.

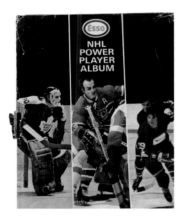

One of my strongest Canadian childhood memories involved Power Players. A friend and I were waiting by the pumps of an Esso gas station at the corner of Sheppard Avenue and Don Mills Road in North York. It was freezing, mid-December, there was a sheet of snow on the ground, and we could see the Christmas lights at Fairview Mall across the way. On the balconies of the rental apartments that surrounded us, tenants had strung together numerous strands of Christmas-tree lights into the shape of seven-storey-high martini glasses. It was one of those inky, dark, silent winter nights that you only get in Canada. Falling snow made cones of light from the streetlights above.

I was starting to lose feeling in my toes in my moon boots. My GWG jeans were frozen solid and my checked bomber jacket was starting to let in the cold. My Toronto Maple Leafs toque was the only thing keeping me in the game.

We hid behind the gas pumps so that the attendant couldn't see us. He was inside, watching the Leafs game, surrounded by delicious silver bags of Hostess ketchup-flavoured potato chips. I had a Cherry Blossom chocolate bar (yes, chocolate bar, not candy bar) in my coat for the walk home later.

A car pulled up and the driver bought gas. The attendant left, and before the car pulled away, we descended on the car.

"Hey, sir, do you have kids?"

The driver answered, "No, why?"

"Can we have your Power Players?" Can we have your Power Players. That winter, I must have asked, "Can we have your Power Players?" at least a hundred times.

The driver handed over his stack of Power Players, and before he drove off, he said, "Hold on, boys." He reached into his glove compartment and gave us another forty stacks of Power Players. We bolted home, and in the sugar rush of my Cherry Blossom and the safety of my family's warm apartment, we filled up our Power Players album. I still have it.

Even in December of 1970, at the age of seven, I knew that during that moment at the Esso station, I was having a Canadian experience. Although I had nothing to compare it to, I felt Canadian. A pride came over me.

———

The spirit of the Next Great Nation era extended to industry. In 1968, under the Trudeau government, Canada got into the nuclear reactor business. The government had subsidized the major technological achievement of building the CANDU nuclear reactor. I always thought it was ironic that a country that struggled with entrepreneurship had thrown its hat into such a complicated business and called those reactors, of all things, CANDU. America was a "can-do" country; Canada was a "might-do" country. Unfortunately, it's theorized that the CANDU reactor may be where Pakistan got its nuclear weapons program from, but that's for another book. (Sorey, eh?)

In 1969, Montreal once again did us right by getting the first Canadian team in Major League Baseball, the Montreal Expos. The name, of course, was an homage to the highly successful Expo 67. Everything about the Expos franchise was not American. From the name, to the softball-style uniforms, to the multi-coloured caps, all the way to the weird *M* logo. The Expos had their first franchise player in Daniel Joseph "Rusty" Staub, a right fielder with bright red hair. Staub made the classy choice of learning French, and the French Canadian Montreal fans responded with delight, giving him the nickname *le Grand Orange*.

I remember watching Expos games on Toronto's French-language CBC channel, CBLFT. The French translations for baseball terms were awesome. For example, baseball was *le baseball*. The batter was *le frappeur*, a baserunner was *un coureur*. A foul ball was *une fausse balle*, a fly ball was *un ballon*, a pop-up was *une chandelle*, an infield pop-up was *une mini-chandelle*. My favourite was the French term for a sacrifice bunt: *un amorti sacrifice*. It sounds like a cross between a suicide pact and an orgasm.

In the 1968 Winter Olympics, Canadian skier Nancy Greene won a gold medal, an event so rare that she was hired to do a commercial for Mars bars. In the commercial, Nancy Greene is in front of her trophy case, and someone teases her. In her thick Canadian accent, she says "Hey, no-oh jo-ohking in the tro-ohphy room." We thought it was the most Canadian sentence in the world.

Thirty-two years later, my brother Paul visited me in L.A. and teased me about my Teen Choice Award, which was a full-sized surfboard. Reflexively, I said, "Hey, Paul. No-oh jo-ohking in the tro-ohphy room, eh?" You can take the boy out of Canada . . .

In September 1969, it was Toronto's turn to give Canada some glory when it held the Toronto Rock and Roll Revival festival, featuring the Doors, Alice Cooper, Little Richard, and surprise guests John Lennon and Yoko Ono. John and Yoko's performance as the Plastic Ono Band was recorded and released that December. It was the first live album released by any member of the Beatles (together or separately). This is the concert where Alice Cooper famously threw a chicken into the crowd, which then, in turn, ripped the chicken apart and threw it back at him. That incident stole many of the headlines, despite the presence of John and Yoko. But for me, I was thrilled that John chose Canada.

In December 1969, John Lennon and Yoko Ono returned to Toronto to start their famous "War Is Over" campaign. In an attempt to end the Vietnam War, the Lennons had decided to use their celebrity to sell the concept of peace as if it were a product. They had hoped to begin their advertising-style protest in New York, but because of a trumped-up marijuana charge and a personal vendetta by Richard Nixon, John and Yoko were unable to get into America. So, as an alternative, John and Yoko chose Toronto with the help of Australian-born rock journalist and producer Ritchie Yorke. Ritchie was a tireless promoter of Canadian rock and one of the architects of CanCon. Thank you, Mr. Yorke.

The simple poster for the War Is Over campaign was designed by University of Toronto students, who also donated their time to post the posters all over Toronto. Ultimately, the campaign, which started in Toronto, had billboards all around the world.

I found out about the War Is Over protest in a traumatic way. On what was possibly the coldest day of my life, in December 1969, my brothers and I were tobogganing. Over the perpetual hum of the 401, we heard a buzzing sound in the sky. It was a skywriter spelling out the word WAR.

A little background into the Canadian psyche: Canadians had the misguided belief that America was preoccupied with invading Canada. It was only years later, when I lived in America, that I realized that Americans view the Great White North not so much as a country but more, as the popular meme suggests, as "America's hat."

After seeing WAR spelled out in the sky, my brother Paul came to the conclusion that, indeed, the Americans were invading. I began to cry uncontrollably out of

Ritchie Yorke is a Canadian hero who happens to be Australian. He is a great man of peace who helped put the Canadian music industry on the map. I hail you, Ritchie.

133

The Number One
Canadian Best Seller

ULTIMATUM

OIL OR WAR?

RICHARD
ROHMER

terror. Every night, we had seen the Vietnam War on television, and now it seemed, Canada was next.

The skywriter then spelled IS OVER. My brother Peter said, with certainty, "War is over Canada right now. When we get home, we'll have hot chocolate and begin to form resistance cells."

Now it spelled out WAR IS OVER IF YOU. Peter said, "All right, here comes the ultimatum. Obviously, it's 'if you don't give us your oil.'" Peter shouted to the sky, "Bring it on, you Yankee buggers!" I continued to weep. As we marched home, the skywriter completed the message. It read, WAR IS OVER IF YOU WANT IT HAPPY XMAS LOVE JOHN + YOKO. My crying changed from tears of fear to tears of pride. John Lennon and Yoko were in Toronto. They had personally sent Toronto a Christmas card in the sky. Later that week, we watched John Lennon and Prime Minister Trudeau hanging out in Ottawa. John thought our prime minister was cool. I couldn't help but feel the reason John chose Canada was that he knew what we knew: Canada was going to be the Next Great Nation.

And if this nation was to be great, it needed to be fit. In the late 1960s it was observed that the average thirty-year-old Canadian had the same level of fitness

Opposite: Richard Rohmer's novel tells of a U.S. invasion of Canada, set against the energy crisis of the 1970s. Rohmer, a former Royal Canadian Air Force officer, has Canada defeat the Americans using the element of surprise. I read this book thirty times.

135

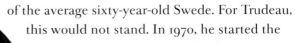

of the average sixty-year-old Swede. For Trudeau, this would not stand. In 1970, he started the ParticipAction program, which was a government initiative to raise the fitness level of the nation. At school, ParticipAction created the Canada Fitness Test. Every child had to go through a series of physical tests and actions to determine their level of fitness, and they were issued an embroidered patch that let any and all know how they had performed.

The highest performers received an Award of Excellence; below that was gold, then silver, and then the lowly bronze. My brain told me I was going to get the Award of Excellence. My body quickly informed me that I was to receive silver. People who won the Award of Excellence tended to put that patch on their denim jacket. We silvers tended to pretend that the patch had fallen through a sewer grate. Having said that, I still have my silver patch. I would have gotten gold, but I stumbled on the shuttle run. I don't have to think about that anymore, right?

While Canada was getting fit, domestic issues took centre stage. In 1970, Prime Minister Trudeau had to deal with war and violence right here at home in Canada. Canada has always been a nation of two solitudes: English Canada, which comprises the vast majority in nine of the ten provinces, and French Canada, which is the predominant culture of the province of Quebec. The two traditions had forged an uneasy coexistence since the battle at the Plains of Abraham. Quebec was Catholic, English Canada mostly Protestant. United by hockey, divided by language.

In the 1960s, a Quebec separatist movement was slowly growing; although called the Quiet Revolution, there was some violence and loss of life in the form of bombings and armed robberies. I remember seeing mailboxes welded shut in Toronto as a way of combatting the rash of mailbox bombings.

In 1970, the Quiet Revolution got loud. In what is known as the October Crisis, a Quebec separatist terrorist organization called the *Front de libération du Québec,* or FLQ, kidnapped a British trade minister named James Cross and the deputy premier of Quebec, Pierre Laporte. In response to these kidnappings, a week later, Prime Minister Pierre Trudeau invoked what is known as the War Measures Act, giving the federal government sweeping powers of search and seizure and placing restrictions on freedom of the press. Literally overnight, Canada went from a democracy to a dictatorship. There were soldiers and tanks in the streets of Canada. When the press asked how far Prime Minister Trudeau would go with his suspension of civil liberties in order to defeat the FLQ, he responded, "Just watch me."

Just watch me. Is this the mealy-mouthed language of a "weak progressive"? No. It was pure Trudeau.

Trudeau's harsh, draconian response to the FLQ crisis seemed, to many, to be out of character for a progressive liberal, except to those who had read Trudeau's writings on the nature of governance. Unlike many Conservatives who want to appear to be tough on matters of law and order, Trudeau actually was ruthless—not in the interest of offering red meat to the "law and order" set, but because the FLQ infuriated his sensibilities about the sanctity of the democratic process. Yes, of course he found the violence of the FLQ repugnant, but what he found equally repugnant was the FLQ's barbaric defiling of the sanctity of democratic choice, whereby authority is granted only to the elected, the just, and the competent, and not to hoodlums, bullies, or fascists.

After Prime Minister Trudeau refused the FLQ's demands, Pierre Laporte was apparently executed (though later it would be revealed that he was accidentally killed in a struggle). James Cross was released, fifty-eight days after his kidnapping, and although several of his captors were granted their freedom in exchange (six were later convicted upon their return to Canada), the FLQ was effectively destroyed. True to Prime Minister Trudeau's word, the Bill of Rights and our tradition of democracy were restored.

For a seven-year-old, the crisis was both terrifying and thrilling. Before the October Crisis, I had never seen a Canadian soldier on the street, and up until then I wasn't aware that we even had tanks. When the newspapers showed the bloody remains of Pierre Laporte in the trunk of a car, I was horrified. For many years afterward, my brother Paul "Makeshift Morgue" Myers would wince every time my dad opened the trunk of our car, expecting to find Pierre Laporte . . . again. In the schoolyards of North York, our tension was transmuted into a macabre game in which you would get sucker-punched in the back of the head, and when you turned around to see who hit you, the offender would simply say, "FLQ." And then, in turn, you would "FLQ" somebody else. I had a bruise in the middle of my back, and when my mum asked me where I got it, I said, "FLQ." My mum misheard that to be "Fuck you," and she clocked me in the back of the head. We didn't quite know what FLQ meant, but we knew it was bad. We also knew that Trudeau had protected us.

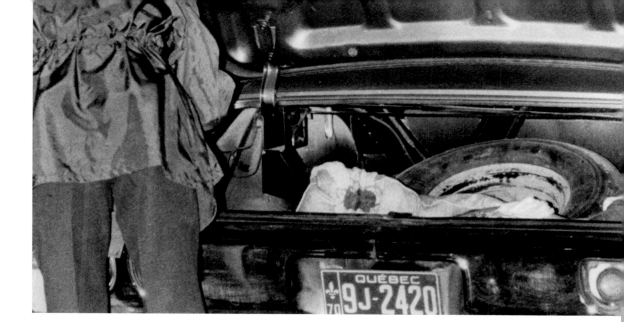

It's the body of Pierre Laporte. In many ways the FLQ crisis was our 9/11. A very scary time in Canada.

My favourite Trudeau memory is the now-legendary "fuddle duddle" scandal. During Question Period, on the very formal floor of the House of Commons in Ottawa, Prime Minister Trudeau, in response to some particularly personal taunting, flipped a member of the Opposition the bird and mouthed the words "Fuck off." This was seen by everybody in the House. It was like CSPAN "After Hours," and the press went crazy.

They asked Trudeau, "What were you thinking . . . when you moved your lips?"

Trudeau responded, "What is the nature of *your* thoughts, gentlemen, when you say 'fuddle duddle' or something like that? God, you guys . . ." And then he walked off.

He was caught saying, "Fuck off," and he claimed to have said, "Fuddle duddle." That is a big set of nuts. The next day, a Canadian candy company put out a form of toffee called Fuddle Duddle with a caricature of Trudeau on the label.

139

Trudeau inspired us. We may not have had an interesting past, but we were sure as hell going to have an interesting future. Canada became future-crazy. There was even a very forward-thinking show about futurism called *Here Come the '70s* that was shot in Toronto, and it featured a theme song played on a Moog synthesizer. *Here Come the '70s* holds up to this day, not only in its prescience, but as a fascinating artifact of a time when futurism was a current concept and not something we now find ourselves nostalgic for.

By this point, Marshall McLuhan had moved back to Canada and was continuing his then controversial, pioneering study of mass media at the University of Toronto. It was here that he wrote *From Cliché to Archetype*. Under McLuhan, this new field of media studies eschewed the tired orthodoxy of print in favour of the new electronic media of television and satellite broadcasts. Though he spoke of the world as a "global village," his futuristic revolutionary work was not being done in Paris or New York but in Canada.

Downtown Toronto, in the spirit of "new is better than old," was going through a radical change: every day, another new, modern building. To make room for these new buildings, Toronto tore down many of its more beautiful, historic buildings. In its place were lots of concrete, jagged lines, as if inspired by Hitler's

Atlantic Wall or the Luftwaffe's flak towers that ringed Berlin. In Toronto, at this time, the wrecking-ball business and the concrete industry were booming and we're still paying the architectural price. Some old buildings survived because they were being repurposed.

The Victorian houses were being made into neo-Victorian clothing stores. Toronto had embraced the new trend of psychedelia, and I remember going downtown, to Yorkville, "to see the hippies," and feeling proud that Toronto had hippies. People were swimming nude in the Don River. We literally saw "barenaked ladies." We had arrived.

I REMEMBER GOING DOWNTOWN, TO YORKVILLE, "TO SEE THE HIPPIES."

In 1971, not everyone rejected the old; the great Canadian historian Pierre Berton captured the fervour surrounding the Next Great Nation era with his smash hit book *The Last Spike*. Berton was the Ken Burns of his time, and *The Last Spike* told the story of the Canadian Pacific Railway. Pierre Berton is a hero to me. He taught us that we do have stories to tell. I used to love seeing him on Canadian TV and hearing him talk about the otherwise dry story of Canada in such an interesting way. He was . . . calming.

Equally calming was the 1972 TV series *The Beachcombers*, starring Bruno Gerussi. It was set in British Columbia, and it was about a coastal community that had to deal with the scourge of driftwood. I watched *The Beachcombers* every day after school for many years, and yet, I still cannot tell you what happens in any individual episode. *The Beachcombers* is inexplicable to non-Canadians. I shall not attempt to explain it. I have one word for you: YouTube. (Though that is really two words stuck together.)

Perhaps the most defining moment of the Next Great Nation era is the 1972 Summit Series, an eight-game hockey tournament between Canada and the Soviet Union.

For me, the story of the Summit Series really comes down to three moments when we felt that this hockey tournament was further proof of Canada's inevitable emergence. The first was "The Speech," the second was "The Chant," and the third was "The Goal."

I warn you that I cannot be a dispassionate historian when it comes to the '72 series. This was very personal for me, and very meaningful and joyful. I love the game of hockey—how it looks, how it sounds, and in the good old days when Maple Leaf Gardens was still around, how it smelled, from the smell of the Gardens' over-salted popcorn, to the smell of overly strong cologne, to the smell of electricity from the dubious, rickety escalators. I even remember the smell of the urinal pucks in the men's room. And by the way, who takes a dump at a hockey game? But people definitely did, believe me. I guess, it was a case of dump and chase . . . but again, I digress.

Hockey, for me, is . . . home.

When we all heard that the series was going to happen, my brothers and I, like the rest of the country, thought it was going to be a cakewalk for Canada. We had seen the hilarious training films of the Soviets on *Hockey Night in Canada*, which showed them practising with oversized weighted sticks and parachutes on their backs when they ran suicide drills. It was the typical Soviet medicine ball–throwing exhibition-of-science-and-strength crap (think *Rocky IV*). My God, were we smug. We even felt a little bad for them, because they had drab C.C.C.P. uniforms and weird Jofa helmets that made them look like evil robots (ironically, Canada's greatest player, Wayne Gretzky, would later wear a Jofa helmet).

My brothers and I saw Game 1 in eighty-degree weather on a colour television in the Better Living Centre building at the Canadian National Exhibition. On the way to the CNE, we saw a billboard for a Canadian vodka company called McGuinness Vodka. It read, in reference to the Soviets, "If they can play hockey, we can make vodka." This was going to be funny.

By the end of Game 1, which Canada lost, 7–3, it wasn't at all funny. A week later, in a stroke of advertising brilliance, McGuinness vodka had changed its billboard by crossing out the "If," so that it now read, "they can play hockey, we can make vodka." And boy, could they play hockey. They were great skaters—fit, disciplined, and they had weird, Harlem Globetrotter–type plays where they literally skated in circles around the Canadian team, who looked . . . hungover. And, worst of all, those Ruskies could stickhandle. Somehow, stickhandling felt like a Canadian skill—how dare they?

We won Game 2, we tied Game 3 (a tie? This series was *so* not designed by Americans), and in Vancouver we lost Game 4, 5–3. Some fans in the Pacific Coliseum booed Team Canada off the ice. I, however, was in Toronto, booing those Vancouver fans. This brings us to Moment Number 1, "The Speech." Phil Esposito, an alternate captain of Team Canada, gave the most rousing postgame speech on nationwide TV:

> Every one of us guys, thirty-five guys that came out and played for Team Canada, we did it because we love our country, and not for any other reason, no other reason. They can throw the money, uh, for the pension fund out the window. They can throw anything they want out the window. We came because we love Canada. And even though we play in the United States, and we earn money in the United States, Canada is still our home, and that's the only reason we come. And I don't think it's fair that we should be booed.

Esposito's speech made me proud to be Canadian, and I couldn't help but think that a speech like that would never have happened before 1967. The Next Great Nation initiative was working.

Game 5 was in Russia, and Canada lost, 5–4. The series was 3–1, with one tie, in favour of the U.S.S.R. This leads me to Moment Number 2: "The Chant," which happened in Game 6. There were three thousand Canadian fans who had travelled to Moscow, and the Soviets had seated them all together. The Soviet Union, of course, was a country in a permanent state of the War Measures Act. In a display of defiance and patriotism, the Canadian fans came up with a chant: "*Nyet, nyet, Soviet! Da, da, Canada!*" They could have been thrown in jail for this. I still can't get "*Nyet, nyet, Soviet! Da, da, Canada!*" out of my head, and that

was forty-four years ago. Canada eked out its first win in Russia, bringing the series to 3–2, still in favour of the U.S.S.R., with two games remaining.

In Game 7, Canada won, 4–3, evening up the series. It all came down to Game 8. I was nine years old, school was back in session, and just like when the Americans landed on the moon, we were all taken to the gym to watch *the* game on three Canadian-made Electrohome televisions that were on these tall, wheeled stands. The gym was packed. We were given little Canadian flags. All of us kids were amped, as if we had all had ten Cherry Blossom chocolate bars and a six-pack of Dominion Cola.

Soviets up 1–0.

Esposito ties 1–1

First period ends 2–2.

Soviets up 5–3 by the end of the second period.

Esposito saves a goal, and then goes on to score to make it 5–4 for Russia.

Yvan "The Roadrunner" Cournoyer scores to tie it at five.

And this brings us to Moment Number 3: "The Goal." As Paul Henderson puts it, "I jumped on the ice and rushed straight for their net. I had this strange feeling that I could score the winning goal." The Canadians advanced, and with thirty-four seconds left, the great Canadian hockey announcer Foster Hewitt described it: "Cournoyer has it on that wing. Here's a shot. Henderson made a wild stab for it and fell. Here's another shot. Right in front. They score! Henderson has scored for Canada!"

In the gym, coats went flying. Henderson, who played for the Toronto Maple Leafs, had scored the winning goal. Canada had beaten the Soviet Union.

Canada had taken on the mighty Russian bear by itself, and won. Teachers were crying and hugging. Parents spontaneously came to pick up their children. I was the last to leave the gym, and as the AV squad closed the metal doors on the Electrohome televisions to put them away in the AV closet, I sat on my coat by myself and prayed, "Please, God, never let me forget this moment." If we could beat the Soviets, we could do anything. We were number 1. No more number 2. There was no going back. Maybe we were already the Next Great Nation. But, alas, there was more building to come.

Specifically, the world's tallest building, the CN Tower. In 1973, the Canadian National Railway, or CN, began building a tower on its property in downtown Toronto, for the purpose of transmitting radio and TV signals. It was to be the world's tallest building, but in typical fashion, Canadians feel compelled to describe it more accurately as the world's tallest free-standing structure. It was completed in 1976, and I remember watching with great pride as a Sikorsky lift helicopter put the last piece of the tower in place. My parents bought souvenir CN Tower whisky. The whisky was polished off right away, but we kept the bottle. I still have it.

In the shadow of the new CN Tower, across the street from where John Lennon had performed at the 1969 Rock and Roll Revival

147

festival, there was a dance studio called the Roland and Romaine School of Dance. It was run by the choreographers of a Canadian TV variety show called *The Pig and Whistle*, which was set in a mock-English pub and featured English-oriented entertainment. The dancers did the sort of cheeky-chappy dancing you would see in *Mary Poppins*.

I told my parents that that's what I wanted to do for a living, and they, to their credit, enrolled me in the Roland and Romaine School of Dance. I took tap dancing lessons there. My ever-supportive brothers decided, much to my horror, that my new nickname should become Twinkletoes. I owe a debt of gratitude to the nickname, because it was how I learned to fist-fight.

One day, I got a call from Romaine (I never really knew her name). A company producing a television commercial was looking for child dancers. They asked

if I wanted to audition, I said yes, and, to my surprise, I got hired. It was a commercial set in the fifties, and a young family broke into dance. I was the son; I had a sister, a father, and a mother, who was played by Gilda Radner. Gilda had not yet been hired for *Saturday Night Live* (in fact, *Saturday Night Live* didn't exist yet).

It was a four-day shoot, and I, like every other human being who met her, fell in love with Gilda. And on the last day of the shoot, we said our goodbyes in the parking lot. I cried like a baby. My whole family came to pick me up, and upon seeing me crying, my brothers gave me a new nickname to replace Twinkletoes. I was hereby called Sucky Baby, because of the emotion I had displayed upon my cruel separation from Ms. Gilda Radner, who became known in my house as "your girlfriend." I was Sucky Baby for ten years. Even in my twenties, if I displayed any intellectual precociousness, I was immediately brought down to earth with "Wow, that's really smart, Sucky Baby." I went on to do about seventeen commercials, and several movies made for TV (thanks, CanCon!). And in the process, I ended up working with Bruno Gerussi, Lee Remick, and Lois Maxwell, who played Moneypenny in the James Bond movies.

One day in 1975, I came home and my brother said to me, "Hey, Sucky Baby, your girlfriend [Gilda Radner] is gonna be on this stupid show on Saturday. It's a live comedy show that doesn't even have a name. It's just called *Saturday Night*." That week, Saturday came and we gathered around the television. Our minds were blown. This was a show unlike any other show we had ever seen. It was rock and roll. It was dangerous. It was created by a Canadian! Lorne Michaels! I had been a fan of Lorne's since 1970, when I saw him on his CBC comedy show with Hart Pomerantz, *The Hart and Lorne Terrific Hour* (thanks again, CanCon). Gilda entered one of the sketches and I fell in love with her all over again. As the cast gathered onstage for the closing credits, a feeling came over me, and in an outrageous act of unearned confidence, I turned to my brothers and said, "I'm going to be on that show one day." My brothers were immediately encouraging: "Yeah right. Dream on, Sucky Baby."

> SATURDAY CAME AND WE GATHERED AROUND THE TELEVISION. OUR MINDS WERE BLOWN.

Here was the coolest show on American TV, created by a Canadian, co-starring Dan Aykroyd. These are the fruits of the dreaded big government. In fact, a case could be made that American big government also played a hand in the creation of *Saturday Night Live*. *SNL* owes as much to the CBC as it does to FDR and the WPA. And here's the link: Franklin Delano Roosevelt, under the New Deal, created the Works Progress Administration (WPA), which was a make-work project during The Depression. The WPA hired

Lorne Michaels and Hart Pomerantz on their CBC show, *The Hart and Lorne Terrific Hour*. Another great reason to give thanks for CanCon.

a dramatist, Viola Spolin, to teach immigrant children English through the use of improvisational theatre games. Viola Spolin's son, Paul Sills, brought these improv games to Chicago in the 1950s, and he, with David Shepherd, formed the improv sketch troupe the Compass Players. Enter Mike Nichols, Elaine May, and Bernie Sahlins, and thus the Second City Theater Company was born. The Second City franchised to Toronto, where a young Lorne Michaels met Gilda Radner, Dan Aykroyd, and, in Chicago, John Belushi and Bill Murray. They formed the nucleus of the Not Ready For Prime Time Players, and *Saturday Night Live* was born. No FDR? No *SNL*.

The Next Great Nation era reached its climax at the 1976 Montreal Olympics. It was the first Olympics after the Munich Massacre, and the flamboyant mayor of Montreal, Jean Drapeau, had a lot riding on its success.

Trouble began to brew before the Games even started, when construction fell behind schedule and ran way over budget, despite Mayor Drapeau's overconfidence in 1970 when he declared, "The Olympics can no more have a deficit than a man can have a baby." The Games started on schedule, though there were construction problems throughout. And, thankfully, there was no bloodshed, but Canada performed miserably, becoming the only host country in the history of the Olympics not to earn a gold medal. In fact, when Canadian broadcasters changed the film that ran alongside the national anthem at the end of the broadcast day, they included a clip of the 1976 Montreal Olympics: Canadian high jumper Greg Joy successfully clearing the bar. What's not made clear in the footage is that Greg Joy only won a silver medal. Imagine the Americans putting a silver medal winner in a montage like this. And in an ironic twist, Greg Joy was actually born in the States.

The 1976 Montreal Olympics racked up a one-billion-dollar debt that took thirty years to pay off. In 1977, Mayor Drapeau gave birth to a beautiful baby boy.

For Canada, 1976 was a foreboding year after what had felt like a fantastic roll since Expo 67: we'd had the Centennial, Trudeau, John Lennon, CanCon, the '72 Summit Series, a flourishing culture, and national pride was at an all-time high. But had the wave crested?

We had come so close. Would Canada ever get a mission statement? An identity?

Mike at 19
Oct. 82

CHAPTER FOUR

A Canadian Adulthood

Top: Me and my Mountie, "Don," in my first apartment in Parkdale. Note the denim shirt, part of my Canadian tuxedo.

Right: Not to "luck-shame," but why was his toe sticking out like that, begging to be rubbed?

IN THE SUMMER OF 1982, I was 19, and I had just been hired by the Second City Theater Company. I moved out of my family's home in Scarborough and got my first downtown apartment, which was in a rundown west-end Toronto neighbourhood called Parkdale. I had a room in a giant Victorian mansion filled with conceptual artists. My brother Paul lived there as well, and he introduced me to a world of artists and artistic sensibilities and the music of Brian Eno and Talking Heads. The artists in this house all had Canada Council art grants, and I would hardly say they

155

The Second City Touring Company Van, aka "The Van." The smell of stale costumes, cheese popcorn, Tuborg beer, and alcohol flasks—it could be a bit cultish.

156

were living in the lap of luxury. It was subsistence living, but it was cool.

Each day, I would take the streetcar all the way to the centre of town. At Queen and Yonge, I would go into the Eaton's department store and, for good luck, I would rub the toe of the statue of Timothy Eaton, the store's founder. His toe was brightly polished from other people rubbing it, and it stuck out over the plinth that the statue stood on, as if inviting you to rub it.

I needed luck, because I didn't know what the hell I was doing. My fellow performers in the Second City touring company were seasoned veterans. Each of them was insanely talented. The first part of the show was scripted, usually tried-and-true sketches from the vaults of Second City in Toronto and Chicago.

Performers at Second City tended to fall under various archetypes: the Big Guy (John Candy, Chris Farley); the Smart Guy (Bill Murray, Dan Aykroyd); the Irish Girl (Catherine O'Hara, Tina Fey—though she's not Irish); the Jewish Girl (Elaine May, Gilda Radner); and then my archetype, the Small Guy with Lots of Energy. Martin Short was my patron saint.

The second part of the show, the improv set, was where I shone. I wasn't very strong with scripted material, and certainly not scripted material that I wasn't connected to.

At that time, my friend Dave Foley was doing brilliant, almost experimental sketch comedy with the Kids in the Hall. They were great improvisers, but they didn't care much for the form. Dave Foley would often say, "Improv could do with a rewrite." Their material was personal, fresh, and thrilling. They were doing what I wanted to do, but I was very grateful to be in Second City and my mind was blown that being a professional actor was my "job."

We mostly toured the hinterlands around Toronto, and in the summers there was a permanent gig at a lodge near Algonquin Park—a provincial park in Northern Ontario, roughly a quarter of the size of Belgium. This was the beginning of my "Hamburg period." Second City was kind enough to let me be not-very-good for a long time. My fellow performers taught me well—some of them took me under their wing, because I was a chick that had just left the nest, not yet skilled enough to fly.

SECOND CITY WAS KIND ENOUGH TO LET ME BE NOT-VERY-GOOD FOR A LONG TIME.

Amongst the many gifts I received from the Second City touring company was the opportunity to see the rest of Canada. Until then, other than Quebec, I hadn't seen much of the country.

I remember one particularly eventful cross-Canada tour. We went from Newfoundland on the East Coast to Vancouver on the West Coast. Four thousand miles. Newfoundland was beautiful, and my mind was blown by the Newfie accent, so much so that, after the show in St. John's, I went to a nightclub and pretended I was Scottish for a whole evening, ashamed at how boring my Toronto accent was compared to the Newfie brogue.

The next show was in Halifax, Nova Scotia. I love Halifax. I had the best salmon tartare and Caesar salad of my life at one of those eighteenth-century restaurants down by the beautiful harbour. For a city of its size, it always feels like it has as much nightlife as New York. I had one of my best shows of the tour. It was also, however, the spookiest show.

> I HAD ONE OF MY BEST SHOWS OF THE TOUR. IT WAS ALSO THE SPOOKIEST SHOW.

After the scripted portion, I came out to introduce the improv set. The crowd was electric, but as I was onstage explaining something, a deep, resonant, booming voice from the crowd said, "You have wonderful energy, Michael." The voice sounded like Vincent Price—it was otherworldly.

It was so scary that it made the audience laugh. I wasn't famous, so I don't know how "The Voice" knew my name. I said, "Wow! We have a contingency from Hades here this evening."

The Voice continued, "You really do have great energy, Michael." This time, the audience did a collective "Ooooh." He was scary.

I finished the show, and I was backstage talking to a couple of lovely ladies, when The Voice came backstage. It was attached to a man in his forties, six-foot-five, black ringlets of long, flowing hair, heavy black eye makeup, and black clothing. "You really do have wonderful energy, Michael," he said in his booming voice.

The members of my cast scattered. The well-wishers backstage froze in their tracks. I said, nervously, "Thank you . . ."

He continued, "You know, Halifax is one of seven spots around the world that collects energy."

"Oh yeah?"

"So, we are particularly attuned to those that . . . possess . . . energy."

"Right on." At that moment, I noticed a large pendant around his neck. It was an inverted pentagram, the upside-down star shape favoured by devil worshippers. My heart stopped.

"I'll leave you now, Michael. Blessed be, Michael. Blessed be." He didn't walk out of the room so much as hover backwards. People started to genuflect. Strangers came up to me wondering if I was "OK." Of course,

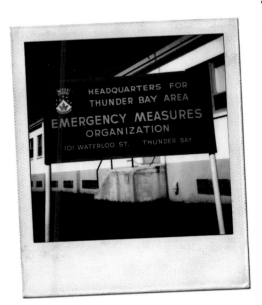

"Blessed be, Michael" became my newest catchphrase with the rest of the cast.

In Thunder Bay, Ontario, the cast conspired to call my room at three o'clock in the morning and every hour afterwards, using devil voices, saying, "Could I speak to Michael, please? I need some of his energy." I would get hand-written messages, slid under the door by hotel staff, that just said, "You have a call from: Blessed be."

159

Thunder Bay is the home of Paul Shaffer, best known as the bandleader on David Letterman's talk show. I spent a day taking Polaroids of Thunder Bay.

SECOND CITY TOURING COMPANY

PRESENTS

"BEST OF SECOND CITY"

I went to the Finnish neighbourhood, where I had a sauna and the Finnish equivalent of a smorgasbord. In the bay is a magical island called the Sleeping Giant, which looks exactly like a sleeping giant.

We then went on to Winnipeg. Winnipeg had more hipsters per capita than any other city in Canada. Home of the world-famous Royal Winnipeg Ballet (government subsidized), the "SoHo" of Winnipeg was an unexpected bohemian delight. Of course, I ate perogies—it's the perogy capital of Canada. I also experienced the corner of Portage and Main, literally the coldest corner in Canada that isn't in the Arctic. Cold. Impervious to the warming effects of several dozen perogies and half a bottle of vodka.

Next, we drove through Saskatchewan—Big Sky country. The flattest place I have ever been. If you stand on a five-step platform, you can see an extra mile. They had to put bends in the road so that people wouldn't fall asleep driving at night. We played a town in Saskatchewan called Swift Current, which the locals call Speedy Creek. After the show, I went to a Native Canadian bar whose house band was called the FBIs, which, upon inquiry, was revealed to stand for the "Fucking Big Indians."

My castmate, though in his thirties, was still a juvenile delinquent. He started to get mouthy and tried to hook me into a fight with the FBIs. I apologized for my asshole Toronto friend, which they accepted. I went outside to get some air. My castmate was given the bum's rush by a Native Canadian who, I swear, was seven-foot-five. My castmate proceeded to steal a cab and implored me to get in, because that would be our ride home. He leaned on the horn, causing the entire bar to empty, including the owner of the taxi. The

castmate hit the gas and left me with these angry locals. The look on my face saved my life, because the entire town burst into spontaneous laughter. They called the cops and invited me in for one more drink and a grilled cheese sandwich. The car was retrieved and the cab driver brought me home.

We went to Regina, Saskatchewan's capital, and had a great show. (Americans never believe that there's a town called Regina.) In fact, in the show, we had a word association scene:

DOCTOR: Mother?

PATIENT: Father.

DOCTOR: Love?

PATIENT: Hate.

DOCTOR: Vagina?

PATIENT: Saskatchewan.

That's the sketch, people. That's it, and it killed, night after night.

And then, in the words of the Guess Who, we went running back to Saskatoon, which, as the name would suggest, is in Saskatchewan. We were two days in Saskatoon. On the free night, I decided to check out the University of Saskatchewan theatre department's year-end production of the Restoration comedy *The Country Wife*. This beautiful theatre at the University of Saskatchewan was packed with Saskatonians. The snobby Torontonian in me had low expectations—it was *Saskatoon*, after all, the sticks. Lo and behold, this little university in the middle of Canada knocked it out of the park. The acting was thrilling, the stagecraft was brilliant, the lighting was artful, student musicians played authentic baroque music live onstage, and it was funny! It was one of the greatest nights of theatre in my life. Thank you, Canadian government. Money well spent.

IT WAS ONE OF THE GREATEST NIGHTS OF THEATRE IN MY LIFE.

That night, I treated myself by staying at the Bessborough Hotel on the Saskatchewan River in downtown Saskatoon. The Bessborough is one of the Canadian railway hotels—huge, majestic, castle-like, with triangular copper roofs, like the Canadian Parliament buildings in Ottawa. Pure Canadiana. One of the nicest hotels I have ever stayed at.

In Calgary, we had another fantastic show. And afterwards, I wanted to go out to experience one of the famous wild bars on Calgary's Electric Avenue. But I was starving, so I went back to the hotel diner on the ground floor. As I took a seat at the counter, I felt a pair of eyes on me. It was a beautiful lady staring at me with such intensity that a sheen of sweat broke out over my forehead. I was with two other cast members who assured me that, due to the bizarre attention I was receiving, I was definitely going to "get lucky" here in Calgary.

She approached. She was stunning. She was French Canadian and said to me, "Allo, Michel. I louved de show."

"Ooh . . . thank you . . . " In my head I screamed, *How does she know my name?!*

"You know, Michel, you 'ave wonderful energy." She spread open her vest, which I hoped might be so that she could show me her ample cleavage. But instead she revealed a pendant. A pentagram, just like that of The Voice in Halifax!

My two cast members got up and ran out of the diner, screaming, "Too much evil! Too much evil!"

Then the beautiful French-Canadian satanist said, "I don' t'ink dey could 'andle your energy." She put her hand on my thigh, which I would later claim left a scorch mark. "Do you want to go to anodder club? I know a great club where you'll feel welcome."

I lied and told her that I was a gratefully recovering alcoholic, and that, should I have one more drink, I would need yet another liver transplant. She left and, as she hit the cold Calgary air, turned back and said to me, "Blessed be, Michel. Blessed be."

I got no sleep.

The next night was Lethbridge, Alberta. We drove past the hoodoos—a unique geological formation of wind-worn rocks that form mushroom-capped columns of stone that create the illusion of a vast army of "rock people" (I'm not talking about the KISS army). I had barely heard of Lethbridge, and I was struck by the variety of terrain in my home and native land.

THEN THE BEAUTIFUL FRENCH-CANADIAN SATANIST SAID, "I DON' T'INK DEY COULD 'ANDLE YOUR ENERGY."

And then we drove through the Crowsnest Pass
in the Canadian Rockies. The Canadian Rockies are
the most beautiful place on the planet Earth, truly
magical, truly virginal, almost a joke. We got to
Nelson, British Columbia, a pristine town nestled
amongst breathtaking mountains, brilliantly pre-
served from its heyday of the Silver Rush (of course,
Canada had a second silver rush in 1976 at the
Montreal Olympics).

We played the art college in Nelson. The audience
was filled with art students, and after the show I got
drunk and started to dance with one of the art tarts at
the school. She was older than me, and very forward—
which, because I was shy, was a godsend. It was a
humid dance floor at the after-show party. Before the
tour, I had bought a new leather jacket. The Art Tart
whispered in my ear seductively, "Do I smell leather?"

I replied earnestly, "Sorry, it's new."

She found my innocence adorable, and whispered,
"Do I smell handcuffs?"

I immediately spit out, "No, you do not smell handcuffs."

Then she said, "Pity. I'm going to get us a drink." She went across the room to her six-foot-five biker boyfriend, and from afar I could see that she was asking him for money to buy me a drink. The biker boyfriend shot me a dagger, so I took off into the next room and hid. Consequently, I missed the troupe van back to the hotel, which was two miles away. I looked in my wallet. I had seventy-five cents. I was going to have to hoof it.

Drunk as a lord, I began to stumble home along the wooded, unlit highway. About a mile in, completely alone, I heard a rustling behind me, and I saw the reflective glow of a wild animal's eye. It was a wolf. My heart started to pound. Then there were twelve wolves. I started to lightly drunk-jog toward the safety of the hotel lights in the distance. All at once, the wolf pack's ears shot up and their nostrils flared, presumably because they too could smell leather. Then they started to jog after me with the princely gait of an accomplished predator. Seeing this, I started to run my fastest. And because of the eleven-plus Molson beer in me, I was now vomitous—or as we say in Scarborough, I had a honk on deck. I started to whimper. So this was how I was going to die . . . torn apart by a pack of wolves in the wilds of British Columbia. At least it would be a Canadian death.

Miraculously, a car with one headlight approached from the other direction. As if out of a 1950s sci-fi movie, I ran to the middle of the road, frantically waving my hands to flag down the car. Mercifully,

> IT WAS A WOLF.
> MY HEART STARTED TO
> POUND. THEN THERE
> WERE TWELVE WOLVES.

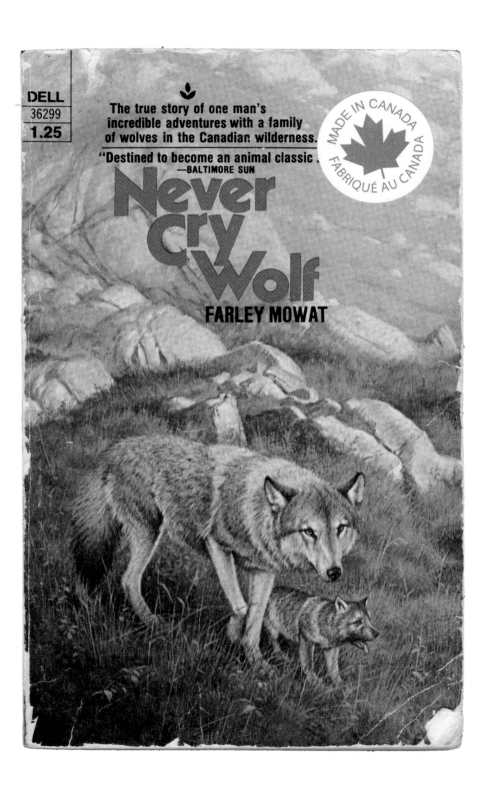

DELL
36299
1.25

The true story of one man's
incredible adventures with a family
of wolves in the Canadian wilderness.

"Destined to become an animal classic . . ."
—BALTIMORE SUN

Never Cry Wolf

FARLEY MOWAT

the one-headlighted car stopped and let me in. To my horror, the driver had one eye. One headlight, one eye. Now I was really freaked out. Were they *his* wolves? Is this how he gets his prey? The conspiracy, of course, would have been confirmed had the wolves only had one eye. He pulled a U-turn to take me to my hotel. Behind us, I saw the faces of disappointed wolves. My cycloptic saviour asked me, "Are you from Toronto?"

I said, "Yeah, how did you know?"

He said, "Only a dipshit from Toronto would walk along this road."

As we arrived at the hotel, the troupe was already loading the touring van to head to the next show. I curled up in the back with the costumes, made myself a little nest, and slept for eight hours.

I woke up in Vancouver. We did a show that night. It was a great house, and as is the case when you're twenty, I was up for going out again. The stage manager of the theatre recommended a bar downtown. Mysteriously, he insisted that the bar was "perfect for me." I wasn't sure if he thought I was gay, or a socialist, or into karaoke, but I went to this "perfect for me" bar with a couple of castmates.

The address took us to an unmarked building with a set of stairs leading down to a basement bar door, behind which we could hear muffled yet slightly sinister music. One cast member said, "Fuck it, Myers, I'm not going in there," and left for the hotel. I opened the door. On the back wall of the bar . . . was a giant pentagram!! The remaining cast members ran away, again shouting, "Too much evil!" On the bar itself was a goat's head. The band was called the 666s. I'm guessing they were the

house band of the beast. I stayed and had a drink. I don't know what possessed me.

I have fond feelings for Vancouver. I got over my grudge about them booing Team Canada during the '72 Summit Series once I remembered that Vancouver was the home of Greenpeace. Good work, Vancouver. Good work, Greenpeace, you do us proud.

Vancouver is stunning. Those two beautiful peaks, the Lions, reminded me of Bruce Cockburn's

"Wondering Where the Lions Are." I love that song, especially his reference to the sweet smell of the fir trees, which I had smelled the night before as I was being chased by wolves. As much as Vancouverites often say they hate Torontonians (why?), Torontonians really love Vancouver. Our love, of course, begins with *The Beachcombers*, but for me, it extends to the Vancouver Canucks' side-stick logo through to the people of Vancouver themselves. Like me, they're very proud to be Canadian.

Well played, Vancouver, well played indeed.

The troupe took the ferry over to Victoria to perform at a theatre festival. Victoria is the architectural proof of the saying that there is no one more English than an Englishman who no longer lives in England. Every Englishman who's been there wishes actual England looked like Victoria. We had arrived in the morning, and as it was a festival of the performing arts, I took the time to broaden my horizons and take in a modern dance performance. I was twenty, always the youngest in the cast, but the dancers in this troupe were all my age or younger. Beyond the beauty of the girls in the troupe, I was struck by the beauty of modern dance itself. A love affair with dance was born that day, and old Twinkletoes here silently vowed to himself to try to include dance in everything he would do.

Hands down, British Columbia is Canada's most beautiful province. Don't tell Toronto, but when people ask, "Where should I go in Canada?" I say British Columbia.

When I got back home to Toronto, a Second City touring company castmate, Christopher Ward, had been offered twelve hours a week of television time on a local Toronto station called CityTV. CityTV had built its reputation by showing pornos on Saturday nights, which they called the *Baby Blue Movie*. Every Saturday, I Jedi mind–tricked my parents into going to bed so that we could watch the *Baby Blue Movie*. So it was no surprise when this maverick station, CityTV, decided to create Canada's version of MTV, with Christopher as its first VJ.

Christopher called me up and asked me to be a guest on his show, *City Limits*, which aired midnight to 6 a.m. on Fridays and Saturdays. I decided to do Wayne Campbell. I would pretend to be Christopher's cousin from Scarborough who had gotten past security and crashed the show. It was successful. So successful that some Canadian viewers complained that they were letting ruffians from Scarborough on Canadian airwaves. They didn't know Wayne was a character—high praise indeed.

IT WAS TIME TO WAKE UP AND SMELL THE DOUBLE DOUBLE.

Christopher is one of my closest friends. He would go on to write the Alannah Myles smash hit "Black Velvet," and he and I would team up again in *Austin Powers*, with Christopher playing a member of Austin's band, Ming Tea.

It was 1984, I had spent two years in the Second City touring company, which was the minor leagues of Second City. The mainstage company was the brass ring, and if you had been in the touring company for as long as I had without a hint of promotion, it was time to wake up and smell the double double: you're not getting promoted. So I quit.

I was twenty-one, and I had no job and no future prospects in Canada. My friends the Kids in the Hall were coalescing into a cutting-edge sketch comedy troupe, but they weren't hiring. I had made a deal with myself that I would never go to either New York or Los Angeles unless I had a job that required me to go there.

Because my parents were English, I could get British citizenship and I could work in England. I had long been a fan of British comedy—Monty Python, Peter Cook and Dudley Moore, and, of course, Peter Sellers. The little voice inside my head said if I didn't move to England now, I never would.

So in 1984 I moved to London and left Canada behind.

———

I had no regrets about leaving Canada. I had been lucky enough to work as a professional actor, and I had gotten to see all of the country. I wondered if Canada would still become the Next Great Nation, as had been promised between 1967 and 1976. And although Trudeau was still my prime minister, I had gotten the sense that the spirit of Confederation, of Expo 67, of the '72 Summit Series, and, frankly, of Trudeaumania itself had become a thing of the past. I held out hopes that Canada would still "make it." Nothing was being said to the contrary. It's just that nothing was being said. And even if Canada did become the Next Great Nation, I wouldn't be there to see it.

Canada is cold, but England is colder. It's a damp cold that gets into your bones, and you are never quite warm. Except if you're in a hot bath, and even then, after ten minutes in a British hot bath, you find yourself cold in a hot bath. My first four months in England were more like an extended vacation, but my Canadian savings were starting to run out, and if I didn't get a job soon, I would have to move back to Toronto with my tail between my legs.

One day, I came across a sign in front of the famous Gate Theatre in Notting Hill. Playing at the Gate for the next three weeks was a sketch-comedy revue called Feeling the Benefit. The cast of Feeling the Benefit were all recent alumni of the Cambridge Footlights. Being a student of English comedy, I knew that the Cambridge Footlights was a theatre club at Cambridge University, which had put on an annual comedy revue since 1883. Past members of the Cambridge Footlights had included my heroes Graham Chapman, John Cleese, and Eric Idle, who went on to form Monty Python. But that was long ago. The cast of Feeling the Benefit was

just a group of young, unknown Footlights graduates who were trying to make a name for themselves by putting on this show. The sign also said that the Gate Theatre was hiring people for the box office, so I went upstairs and got a job working the door at the theatre.

The next day, I showed up to the Gate Theatre for my training. It became clear that I didn't know British currency. There were half-pence coins, one-pence coins, two-pence coins, five-pence coins, twenty-pence coins, fifty-pence coins, and one-pound coins, but also at that time one-, five-, ten-, and twenty-pound notes. Also, there was a thing called concessions. Not a concession stand selling food, but ticket-price concessions for things like old-age pensioners and the unemployed, who needed to show their UB40 unemployment card to get the discounted ticket price. It was the 1980s and Britain had massive unemployment, so most people were on the

dole, which meant long delays as I looked at documents I'd never seen or heard of before.

Because of my Canadian accent, my boss assumed I was mildly delayed. She spoke slowly, over-enunciating, as if I was not only mentally challenged but deaf as well. As if that weren't bad enough, there was a shortage of chairs at the theatre, and so I was forced to sit at the box office table in a prop wheelchair, suffering the unnecessary sympathetic looks of the theatre patrons as I invariably got their change wrong.

I saw Feeling the Benefit. The cast were all young, confident, good-looking, painfully intelligent, and they spoke with posh accents. It was very funny, very clever,

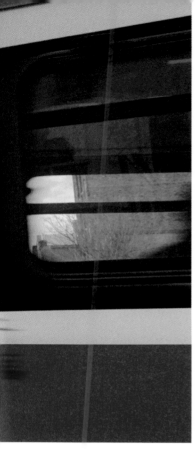

and, to my surprise and delight, very loose and silly. They did amazing American accents. At the end of the show, they did a Quinn Martin–type epilogue, with a perfect American announcer voice saying something like, "Epilogue: Bill Smith was sentenced to twenty-five years in a federal penitentiary. Which is American for jail." It was hard for me to watch the show because I wanted to be onstage performing instead of working in the box office, making ten pounds a night, freezing my ass off in the unheated lobby of the theatre, sitting in a prop wheelchair and watching other people follow their dreams.

The cast was nice. There was one woman in the show, Morwenna Banks, who was fantastic. I would meet her again later in life, when she was briefly on *Saturday Night Live*. But I now hear Morwenna Banks every day, because she's the voice of Mummy Pig in the British children's show *Peppa Pig*, which my three young children are obsessed with. But I digress.

Another cast member of Feeling the Benefit stood out: Neil Mullarkey. He was funny, smart, had a great physicality, and he was very likeable. There are performers you admire, performers you like, and performers you both like and admire. Neil was a performer I both liked and admired. Over the run of the show, I got to know the cast a little, and from time to time, I was able to make them laugh.

Morwenna Banks. I'm a fan and so are my children.

After the show, I would sit in my prop wheelchair, cashing out, and as the cast left to get a drink, I would often shout after them, "Great, walk away! Wish I could!" And then I would roll myself to the top of the stairs and yell down at them, "Must be nice, assholes!" And then,

175

in mock desperation, "Don't leave me!" It would always get a nice laugh, and somehow, it meant more to me that I was getting a laugh from smart English people. But that's just my Canadian low self-image.

On the last night of the three-week run, Neil Mullarkey invited me to join him and the cast for a drink at a pub. I finished cashing out and headed over. Mullarkey asked me how I'd gotten to England, and I told him about Second City. He had heard about Second City and said in his very posh accent, "If you'd been a professional comedian at Second City, why on earth would you come to London?" I told him I wanted to be in the land of Python and Peter Sellers. He said that at the moment, there was a booming alternative comedy scene, which meant there were plenty of places to play. I explained to him the Queen Street comedy scene in Toronto: places like the Rivoli, the Beverley Tavern, and the Cameron House.

He showed me a copy of *Time Out* magazine, the magazine that, amongst other things, listed all the comedy venues in London. There were easily twenty-five places to play. He pointed out that if you got enough material together, you could do two shows a night, every night. I was amazed. He asked me if I wanted to be in a double act with him. The next day, I quit my job at the Gate Theatre.

I started to write material with Neil, but I had no idea whether English audiences would like my comedy. I was also unsure of whether I should perform with a

I WAS UNSURE OF WHETHER I SHOULD PERFORM WITH A CANADIAN ACCENT, OR IF I SHOULD TRY TO ADOPT AN ENGLISH ACCENT.

Canadian accent, or if I should try to adopt an English accent—I could already do Liverpool and Scottish dialects, but that wouldn't match Mullarkey's accent. Using my box office money, I decided I would take three elocution lessons at the Central School of Speech and Drama, to learn Neil Mullarkey's accent, which is the posh southern English accent, like the Queen's, that is called Received Pronunciation. During the first lesson, we went through the twenty-one vowel sounds of Received Pronunciation. Right away, my snobby English speech teacher stopped me and said, "I can't in good conscience take your money."

I said, "Why? What's wrong?"

He said, "You're never going to learn this. It's your horrible Canadian accent. The monotonous drone, the ridiculous overstressing of final *R*s, the grotesque diphthong on the vowel sound of the word *out*. If you spent several lifetimes trying to speak properly, your Canadian nasal twang would fail you every time."

I was devastated, but Scarborough kicked in. As I left his office, I said, "Thank you for your time, but may I ask you one small favour?"

"What?" he said curtly.

I said, "Can you please go fuck yourself? I happen to like my Canadian accent."

Of course, I didn't say that to him. I wish I had. But I did think it, an hour later, while standing on the subway platform. It was a perfect example of the French expression *l'esprit d'escalier*, which means "spirit of the staircase." In France, every building's concierge has a window in the front lobby. As a tired tenant comes home from work, he passes the concierge, who invariably says something snarky. Exhausted, the tenant doesn't have a comeback until halfway up the staircase, far too late for

a timely rebuttal. Thus, a retort come too late is the product of *l'esprit d'escalier.*

What was all the more alarming to me was that I had actually thought that assimilating into Britain would be a breeze for me. I'm of British heritage. Growing up, I ate English foods, listened to English music, watched English TV shows, watched English soccer (Liverpool, of course). My parents had English accents, with my dad having one of the strongest and most recognizable—the Liverpool accent. But nothing makes you feel more Canadian than moving to Britain. Even more than moving to America. We can "pass" in America. Not so in Britain.

British culture is so impenetrable that, during World War II, even the German spy service, the *Abwehr,* were unable to successfully infiltrate British society. How, for example, would you make sense of the word *Leicester?* Would you pronounce it LESS-ter? Or the last name St. John-Stevas? Would you know to pronounce it sin-jin-STEE-vas? The last name Beauchamp is pronounced BEACH-em. *Ich gebe auf!* (I surrender!) In England, the second you open your mouth, you give away all your private information, rather like Facebook today.

Within a few months of living in a West London flat that was so cold you could hang meat in it, it became evident to me that assimilation was impossible and I would have to perform in my "Canadian nasal twang." So Neil Mullarkey and I created material for our imaginatively named double act, Mullarkey and Myers. I would be the Canuck and Neil would be the limey.

The London alternative comedy circuit in the 1980s was a vibrant, cutting-edge, mixed bag of eccentric, experimental, mostly political sketch troupes, singer/

songwriters, and standup comedians. It was very anti-Thatcher and anti-Reagan, very pro–Labour Party. Hugh Grant started on the alternative comedy circuit, as did the cast of the show *The Young Ones*, and Jennifer Saunders, known for her role in *Absolutely Fabulous*.

Pretty much any successful British comedian that you see is likely to have performed at one time on the London alternative comedy circuit.

I was Canadian, not terribly political, and the audiences I played for while in the Second City touring company were genteel by comparison. But I was going to throw my hat into this ring in the form of Mullarkey and Myers. That is, if I could get my hat into that ring. It was no small feat.

In a weird way, my being Canadian was an asset for breaking into the London alternative comedy circuit. There were rules—Canadians love rules, and have a Job-like patience for arcane systems. And London had a system.

In order to get a foothold into the London alternative comedy circuit, new acts, like ourselves, had to get booked in one of the smaller venues, usually clubs above pubs, on the outskirts of town. The crowds were small, typically about ninety people. As a newbie, you got the worst slot: you would have to go on first in front of a cold, not-yet-drunk-enough mob. The promoter would only give untested acts like ours five minutes of stage time, which is not nearly enough time to win over a crowd. And you did all of this for free. If you survived, the promoter asked you back, giving you a ten-minute set, this time for a whopping ten pounds. No venue,

> AS A NEWBIE YOU GOT THE WORST SLOT: YOU WOULD HAVE TO GO ON FIRST IN FRONT OF A COLD, NOT-YET-DRUNK-ENOUGH MOB.

large or small, in the centre of town would even deign to meet you until you could show them proof of bookings you had earned in the hinterland. We clipped out all our Mullarkey and Myers listings from the back of *Time Out* and made photocopies, our calling card.

Mullarkey and Myers's first ten minutes of material had to be geared to quickly winning over a cold, disinterested, political comedy–loving, America-hating crowd.

What we couldn't fix about ourselves, we featured. My Canadian (American-sounding) accent was one of them. In our first sketch I played an over-the-top American character and addressed the audience directly.

The British audience did not know what to make of me, but they knew my accent was authentic—I talked just like Americans in movies. If I was English, I was fantastic at dialects; if I was American, they would be charmingly bemused as to why I was on the outskirts of London, performing my heart out to seventy hipsters in a room above a pub.

We did well. But not always. Sometimes there was nothing you could do to win over an English crowd. Remember, Britain is the home of the soccer hooligan. And British alternative comedy fans didn't just heckle you, they humiliated you. As a Canadian, I didn't know that audiences were capable of humiliating anyone. At Maple Leaf Gardens, if the opposing team scored a clever goal, Leafs fans would give them a polite round of applause. The British pub crowds, on the other hand, wouldn't politely applaud; they wouldn't even just boo you off the stage. They were more creative than that: sometimes they would hum you off the stage, or sing you off the stage, or sarcastically laugh you off the stage.

Me in front of Stonehenge. I hated that haircut. It made me look like Mowgli.

And one time, I was sarcastically encouraged . . . off the stage, with one prick being particularly adept at telling you exactly what you would have hoped to hear, except he was being completely sarcastic. In a loud, interrupting voice, he would say such haunting things as, "You're doing a great job, Mike! You have a real future in comedy. A star is born. Keep it up, boys." He got huge laughs, we got crickets, but my hat was off to him.

In time we gathered more material, playing longer sets and inching our way closer to the West End of London. I was making enough money that I didn't have to move back to my parents' house in Canada, which I took as a victory. I called them and told them I was working in a double act with a comedian named Neil Mullarkey, to which my dad responded, "What, was Bill Shenanigans not available?" At the end of the conversation, he told me he'd "had enough of my Mullarkey."

Once we had enough material written, the days were free for me to sightsee. I went to the British Parliament buildings, to see how they compared to the Canadian ones. Ours are smaller.

Any time I started to feel homesick, I would go to Canada House in Trafalgar Square. They showed hockey games there. Believe it or not, that's where I was the first time I saw Wayne Gretzky play! It was nice to hang out with Canadians, to hear my own accent, and to talk hockey. I casually mentioned to one of the people who worked at Canada House that I was on the alternative comedy circuit. He asked how I was doing for money. I told him the truth: I was getting by, barely. He asked me if I wanted to stuff envelopes there at

My Mountie "Don" made the trip to England.

Canada House. For two days' work a week, I could make seventy-five pounds. It was such an insanely generous overpayment, which I later found out was really an elegant way for Canada House to help out struggling Canadian artists in London. I invited the people of Canada House to come see one of my shows, and as it was their mandate to support Canadian artists in Britain, they actually came! Once again, Canadian government to the rescue.

In their honour, Neil and I wrote a sketch, parodying the movie *On the Town*. In that musical, Gene Kelly, Jules Munshin, and Frank Sinatra are sailors on shore leave in New York City. To send a special thanks to Canada House, Neil and I played two Mounties on shore leave in London. The third Mountie was played by a life-sized standee of a Mountie that we got from Canada House. Part of the fun was trying to have it be an all-singing,

183

all-dancing trio, with one of them being two-dimensional. We changed the lyrics to the song "New York, New York." Instead of "New York, New York, a wonderful town . . . ," we sang:

London, England, ain't lookin' shabby,
Tower bridge, Westminster Abbey.
If you get lost then go ask a . . . babby
London, England, ain't lookin' shabby

After a while, clubs would call *us*. Our fees and stage times doubled. We got booked at this massive club called Jongleurs at the Coronet in South London. It went great. They asked us back. Then we got booked at the Comedy Store in Leicester Square. This was the pinnacle. We were doing nine or ten shows a week, making the equivalent of five hundred dollars a week in cash, which I kept in a shoebox, like a drug dealer.

One of the first things I noticed about the alternative comedy circuit in London was that there was very little improvised comedy. There were a few fantastic troupes, but there was no improv comedy scene, as there had been in Toronto. It occurred to me that there were very few people teaching improv in London at the time. I decided to supplement my income by teaching a class at the Comedy Store. To my delight and surprise, there was a great deal of interest in improv in the London comedy scene, and my classes were filled to the rafters.

WE WERE DOING NINE OR TEN SHOWS A WEEK, MAKING THE EQUIVALENT OF FIVE HUNDRED DOLLARS A WEEK IN CASH, WHICH I KEPT IN A SHOEBOX.

Seeing the huge response to the improv classes, the Comedy Store decided to host a weekly improv night. Mullarkey and I, and several other comedians, founded the Comedy Store Players, the Comedy Store's in-house improv troupe. The houses were light at first, but steadily grew.

This little experiment in improv that I co-founded has been running now for 31 years with the same cast, becoming the longest-running theatre show with the same core cast in the history of the English language. It is in the *Guinness Book of World Records*.

By now, Mullarkey and Myers had enough material to book a theatre at the Edinburgh Fringe Festival. The Edinburgh Fringe Festival is an annual summertime performing-arts festival. Doing well at Edinburgh put you into the next tier—perhaps the BBC would give you a show.

We booked a theatre and made tons of posters, which we flyposted everywhere. We did every possible promotional live show, even managed to get on the radio, and someone at the BBC did a filmed piece about us. We needed some deposit money for the theatre, and we had three-quarters of it. I approached Canada House, and they got us half of the remaining quarter. And, fantastically enough, Ontario House got us the last eighth. More big government! Hooray!

We sold out our two-week run and got a fantastic review in *Time Out* magazine. From there, I got hired to do voices for a couple of BBC Radio series. I was hired to do a Scottish accent for one of them. And in one of the greatest ironies of my life, BBC Manchester paid for my train ticket from London to Manchester and put me up in a hotel so that I could play a character that had a Liverpool accent in one of their radio shows.

Me in *John and Yoko: A Love Story*. I play a Western Union messenger giving John Lennon his deportation papers.

I managed to get a London agent, and I got called to audition for an American television movie being shot in London about John Lennon called *John and Yoko: A Love Story*. It was a small role—a New York Western Union messenger who was so influenced by John Lennon that he dressed exactly like him, granny glasses and all. The scene involved the Western Union messenger giving John Lennon his deportation papers. My agent suggested that I not tell them that I was Canadian, because American producers hated Canadians playing Americans in London productions. The Americans could always sniff out Canadian accents. I decided that I would tell them I was from Upstate New York.

I met with the director, Sandor Stern. In the room were twenty or so production people. As I read my part, Mr. Stern wrote something on a piece of paper. After I finished my audition he held up the piece of paper. There was one word on it: BEEN.

He said, "Read this."

Without thinking, I said, "Bean," using the Canadian pronunciation—not "Bin," the American pronunciation.

"'Bean?' Do you mean 'bin?' Upstate New York, huh? Where?" he asked.

"Way Upstate New York. A little town called Toronto, Ontario."

The entire production staff burst into laughter.

Sandor said, "It's your lucky day, kid. I'm Canadian. You've got the job."

I was working steadily. Mullarkey and Myers was continuing to get a following, and the Comedy Store

Players were consistently getting full houses. One day, I got a call from a reporter at the *Toronto Star*. They wanted to do an article about Mullarkey and Myers. The angle was that a Canadian comedian was taking London by storm. I was doing okay but not quite that good. The article came out right before Christmas, and it was a love letter. (Thank you, *Toronto Star*.)

Coincidentally, I was coming back to Toronto for Christmas. During my phone calls back to Toronto, I began to have suspicions that my father was a little "off." My family did not want to upset me, but they had suspicions that he might actually have Alzheimer's. When he picked me up from the airport, I noticed his driving was "off." My dad sold encyclopedias for a living—he had learned how to drive in the British Army, not just cars, but two-and-a-half-ton trucks. He was an expert driver. Something was wrong. On top of that, when we got back to Scarborough, he missed our exit. And as much as he tried to hide it, he was lost.

On one of the nights on this visit, I went down to the Second City mainstage in downtown Toronto. Many of my friends had by now been promoted to the mainstage, including Dana Andersen, who was a gifted Edmonton-born comedian. He invited me to do the improv set. Because I was now improvising twice a week with the Comedy Store Players in London, my improv skills were sharp. The show's director,

Jeff Michalski, was in the audience. I must have had a good show, because the next day, Jeff Michalski invited me to join the Second City mainstage cast full-time.

This was, at once, my dream come true and a nightmare. I had promised Neil Mullarkey I would go with him, one more time, to the Edinburgh Fringe Festival. And besides, things were heating up for Mullarkey and Myers in London. And Neil was my comedy partner. It was a marriage—not only did I respect Neil Mullarkey as a brilliant comedian, but I had come to love him as a brother. Neil is one of the good guys in a business often filled with not-so-good guys. I didn't want to leave Neil; I loved the work we were doing, I loved the London comedy circuit, and he and I had built something very special together. But my dad was sick. If I went back to London, I knew that the next time I would see my dad would likely be in half a year, and in that time I might be returning to see a man who was half of what he once was. Fuck Alzheimer's.

Ultimately, this made me decide to accept the invitation to join the mainstage cast of Toronto Second City, but I told the producers I had to leave for three weeks in the summer to honour my commitment to Mullarkey and go to Edinburgh. In an act of generosity that I will forever be grateful for, they agreed to let me leave for three weeks in August. Thank you, Andrew Alexander. Thank you for hiring me the first time, the second time, the third time, and for letting me honour my commitment to Neil Mullarkey. You're a class act, Mr. Alexander.

THIS WAS, AT ONCE, MY DREAM COME TRUE AND A NIGHTMARE.

I went back to London to tell Neil that I had to return to Canada for my father. He took it well. He was disappointed, as was I, but he was very happy to know that we would at least have Edinburgh.

I did two shows at the Toronto Second City mainstage. One was called *Not Based on Anything by Stephen King*. For it, I was nominated for a Dora Mavor Moore Award, which is Toronto's Tony Award, and the show won a Dora for Best Musical Revue. Our director was John Hemphill. He had been in the cast when I was in the touring company, and I consider him to be one of the best improvisers to have ever stood on the Second City mainstage. He was also a brilliant director who pushed me and the cast to be the best that we could be. He was hilarious, disciplined, and highly principled. I will always cherish the time we had together, shoulder to shoulder, trying to put together the best possible show, and then afterwards, shoulder to shoulder drinking many Molson Canadians.

Many was the night that John and I, after drinking in legitimate bars, would go to speakeasies, until even they closed, ultimately ending up at the Golden Griddle Pancake House on Jarvis Street, eating silver-dollar pancakes and drinking overly strong coffee, talking about comedy movies that we loved, as the blue of dawn warmed up the summer day. Fantastic memories. Not a care in the world, except that the show would be great. Thank you, John Hemphill.

I would walk home on those blue mornings in Toronto. Never once did I worry about crime. I had the presence of mind to realize what a great thing it is, to live in a safe country. Other countries talk about freedom, but the freedom to walk home at night, knowing that the chances of being attacked are slim to none, is perhaps one of the greatest freedoms. There is also great freedom in living in a culture that isn't particularly angry. But a lack of anger does have its downside. Inversely, necessity, or scarcity, can often be the mother of invention or industry, respectively. Before I left for England, I had a sense that Canada had drifted away from its mission of urgently forging an identity. When I returned from England, an even deeper malaise had set in. Canada didn't seem as Canadian. And in response to that, my work became more Canadian.

I HAD A SENSE THAT CANADA HAD DRIFTED AWAY FROM ITS MISSION OF URGENTLY FORGING AN IDENTITY.

I did Wayne Campbell in this Second City show. He was unabashedly from Scarborough, and I felt that Toronto audiences knew it was authentic to my home borough. John Hemphill had written a song for the show called "Fade Away." It was set to the tune of "Sail Away" by Randy Newman, and it ended the show. The message of "Fade Away" was that Canada was losing its culture, that our culture was being subsumed by American consumerism. It listed all the things that Canadians no longer paid attention to because of the magnetic power of American consumer culture. An American friend of mine came up to see the show and was shocked at how anti-American the song was.

I said, "Didn't you think that we Canadians might have an opinion on you Americans?"

"Not really," he said.

"Well, what do Americans think of Canada?" I asked.

"We don't."

Game, set, and match.

Producers from the CBC saw me at Second City and invited me to do sketch pieces on their show *It's Only Rock & Roll*, a rock-themed variety show—sort of a talk show, sort of a news show. I did two characters on *It's Only Rock & Roll*: once again, Wayne Campbell, which I did as "Wayne's Power Minute" out of a panel van we called "The Shaggin' Wagon"; and a German experimental artist character named Dieter. The producers were pleased, and I was asked to do more and more "Wayne's Power Minute" segments, leading up to hosting the *It's Only Rock & Roll* Christmas special.

My dad's condition, however, was continuing to deteriorate. There was a brief period when my dad was aware that he had this disease. And in the spirit of "How fast can we find this funny?" he insisted on calling it "old-timers" disease. It was the best of times and it was the worst of times. His condition worsened to the point where he no longer recognized me. The Rubicon had been crossed.

I needed to get out of town. I had never been to Chicago before, but I had a vacation coming, so I went to Chicago to see the Toronto Maple Leafs play the Blackhawks at the old Chicago Stadium. One of the Original Six. I wanted to get to the stadium before it was torn down.

Chicago and Toronto have a lot in common. *Toronto* is an Iroquois word meaning "meeting place." *Chicago* comes from the Algonquian, meaning "wild garlic" or "wild onion." The cities are roughly the same size. Both are on a Great Lake. Both have a proud tradition of comedy and, by way of our Chicago brothers, improv comedy. But that may be where the similarities end. In Toronto, the subway would take you to College station, half a block from Maple Leaf Gardens, right next to Toronto's fantastic gay neighbourhood on Church Street. On the other hand, the Blackhawks play in a bad neighbourhood—on the other side of the infamous Cabrini-Green Homes, the housing projects made famous in the 1970s sitcom *Good Times*. I got in a cab and told the driver I was going to Chicago Stadium. He asked me, in his thick Chicago accent, "Ohh mye Gad. Are you shurr? Dat's a pritty skeery plase." This did not bode well. We made our way west, and as we got closer to Cabrini-Green, the cab driver auto-locked the doors, rolled up the windows, and reclined his seat back so far that he was lying down while driving. He sped up to 60 miles per hour and went through a red light! Being Canadian, I didn't want to criticize him, but when he went through a second red light, I spoke up.

"What are you doing?" I asked.

"Snye-purs," he said.

"What? Snipers? What do you mean?"

"See deez buildings? Dey love to snype cabs. Don't wurry about da red lights in dis neighburhood. Dey're just street decoration. If I were you, buddee, I'd get yur head down."

I lay flat on the back seat, and within five minutes I was at the front doors of Chicago Stadium. The building looked exactly like a doppelganger of Maple Leaf Gardens.

The atmosphere was electric. All the fans wore Blackhawks sweaters. I had been warned not to wear

August 13, 1993

I love the Chicago Blackhawks jersey. It's a classic. No wonder every Blackhawks fan owns at least one 'Hawks jersey.

193

my Leafs sweater, but I had to wear it. I was also told not to celebrate if the Leafs scored. Although it almost killed me, caution ruled the day, and I sat on my hands as Wendel Clark potted a wrister from the left side, top shelf, where mama keeps the peanut butter. To my surprise, Blackhawks fans were polite, welcoming, and downright friendly. We Leafs fans pride ourselves on our hockey smarts, but these Blackhawks fans had the knowledge, despite only getting half a page of hockey news in the *Tribune*, as opposed to four pages in the *Toronto Star*. In fact, Toronto has eight pages of hockey news on Tuesdays and Thursdays (heaven). Seeing how hard it was to get to Chicago Stadium, I came away feeling that these 'Hawks fans were true hockey fans. Much respect.

The only grief I got was from a three-hundred-pound Blackhawks superfan who wore every possible piece of Blackhawks merchandise. He was a known regular, shouting out a play-by-play of events on and off the ice in a deep, raspy frog voice with a very thick Chicago accent. As I walked up the aisle, he saw my Leafs sweater and bellowed, "Leafs suck!" When a pretty girl went by, he shouted out, in his frog voice, "Hockey bitch! Hockey bitch!" It was more ridiculous than offensive. The entire section broke into uproarious laughter, including the pretty girl.

It was a far cry from Maple Leaf Gardens, where you could often hear a pin drop. There was an energy in Chicago that, at that time, was lacking in Toronto. I wanted to sample this energy. I wanted to be in the home of the original Second City, where Elaine May, Mike Nichols, John Belushi, and Bill Murray created one of the most dynamic movements of sketch comedy in the history of mankind. It was also the home of Mr. Del Close. Del Close was one of the founding members of Second City back in the 1950s, along with Nichols, May, and Paul Sills. He was older, an ex-junkie, his body covered in track marks, which he called his "track suit." He was a Wicca witch who often asked his students to invoke demons as part of their improv training. Del was one of the Merry Pranksters, a group of experimental artists and hippies who lived in a bus and were based out of San Francisco. Tom Wolfe wrote about the Merry Pranksters in his book *The Electric Kool-Aid Acid Test*. Del was one of the inventors of the Happening, which was an unscripted "event" that ravers would well recognize. He and his partner, Charna Halpern, ran a Chicago theatre called the Improv Olympics. Del didn't just teach improv, he taught creativity. He would have salons at his house, where the nature of creativity was discussed, and creative "happenings" spontaneously manifested. One day, I brought over a deck of hockey cards, and with these cards I read Del's fortune, which I called Canadian Tarot.

Improvising my best spiritualist voice, I said, "As there are four divisions in the NHL, there are four energy quadrants that predict your future. I want you to pull out a card. This will be your defenceman card." He pulled out Ray Bourque. I said, "Ahh, the Ray Bourque card. And I see you've placed it in the Norris Division quadrant. There are many fights in the Norris Division. We call it the Chuck Norris Division. Just as Ray Bourque is a stay-at-home defenceman, you will find yourself doing projects around the house.

HE WAS A WICCA WITCH WHO OFTEN ASKED HIS STUDENTS TO INVOKE DEMONS AS PART OF THEIR IMPROV TRAINING.

Del Close. The man, the legend. The patron saint of improv.

But be careful: his slapshot is hard. Someone you know will turn on you. Don't be a hero. Don't try and block the shot."

He was a heavy smoker, and my reading of him caused him to laugh to the point of a coughing fit. Gaining his respect was one of the highlights of my creative life. For Del, every art form and all parts of living were to be studied and incorporated into improv. One day, Del was giving a workshop. He was talking about how important it is that the performer not believe that they were better than their audience. He felt the audience was always smarter than the person onstage. He told a story of going to the Canadian National Exhibition and finding himself in one of the trade show buildings. He was looking at the mass of people going from booth to booth, like so much human cattle. He had caught himself feeling superior, but then he passed an *Encyclopaedia Britannica* booth where a Liverpudlian man was selling encyclopedias. He said that this Englishman was so funny that it reminded him that a sense of humour is not exclusive to professionals. I raised my hand.

He said, "Can I help you?"

I said, "Yeah. That Liverpudlian selling encyclopedias?"

"Yeah?"

"He's my father."

The rest of the class gave a collective gasp.

I'm serious. This actually happened. Spooooky.

But things like this were everyday occurrences in Del's class. There was an element of magic. Ideas flew around the room, connections were made, synchronicity was rife. Del's classes had an almost hive-mind quality. And it was intoxicating. And it wasn't Toronto, where my dad was. Or wasn't.

So I applied for a transfer from Toronto Second City to Chicago Second City. The owner of Second City Toronto, Andrew Alexander, and his Chicago counterpart, Bernie Sahlins, were kind enough to grant that request. My entry into Chicago Second City mainstage was not an easy one. There was much resistance. One Chicago cast member took me to lunch to "be my friend" by informing me that I was not welcome in Chicago; that the cast, whom I had only briefly met, resented my foreign intrusion; and that my Toronto Second City style of improv and comedy, which emphasized character and observation, didn't jive with the superior political satire tradition of the "senior" Chicago mainstage. I wasn't used to this type of psych-out aggressive behaviour. Comedy in Canada and Britain is not a macho affair. Canadian comedy is much more self-deprecating. I had heard stories of Bill Murray diving into the crowd of Second City in Chicago and having fist fights with hecklers. We didn't do that in Toronto.

On my third week at Second City Chicago, it was a particularly cold day and we were rehearsing in the empty, freezing theatre. I had only one sweater, which my beloved Aunty Molly had knitted for me. I wore it so much that it had a hole in it. At one point in the rehearsal, one huge Chicago castmate interrupted me and said, "Nice sweater . . . Why don't we all pitch in and get Myers a new sweater?"

I said, "Why don't we all pitch in and get this fucking asshole some manners?" There was an uneasy, hushed *oooooh* from the rest of the cast. I don't know where my quick response came from—probably Scarborough. In Scarborough, you have to be fast, you have to be funny, or you have to be ready to fight. I was transported back

to the Toronto subway platform at Kennedy station—the end of the line.

Later that night, I was onstage, improvising a scene about world affairs. I played a stuffy British diplomat, who made three—I thought reasonable, and not terribly controversial—statements. In my Brit character, I said, "The Kennedys were rum runners to Canada," "Canada won the War of 1812," and "The Americans dropped the atomic bomb on the Japanese, not to bring Hirohito to heel, but to scare the crap out of the Russians as an opening salvo of the Cold War." Some members of the audience took mock offence at these remarks, but overall my British character was well received, getting some nice laughs.

When I got backstage, that same huge Chicago cast member pinned me against the wall, screaming, "How dare you come to this country, take an American job, and take a shit on America?" I was shocked. Wasn't Second City a bastion of Democratic politics? Wasn't this the theatre that the rioters from the 1968 Democratic National Convention ran to as sanctuary from Mayor Daley's "pigs"? This dude was huge. And I was cornered. I realized that I was in a physical fight, and once again Scarborough came to the rescue.

In my thickest Canadian accent, I said to him, "Hey, buddy, get your fucking hands off me! Or there's gonna be two sounds: my Canadian fist breaking your ugly American jaw, and your Yankee head hitting the fucking floor."

"Oh yeah, jagbag?"

I said, "Jagbag? What the fuck is a jagbag? You Chicago pricks can't even swear right! I'm Canadian, asshole. I've been in thousands of hockey fights. I don't give a fuck how big you are, I'm gonna fuck you up hockey-style." For the record, I'd never been in a hockey fight. But it worked. He let me go. He would've killed me. In my head, I thought, *Did I almost get in a brawl? We're doing comedy, people.* I hate fighting, but my Liverpool dad had always said, "You only fight to get out of a fight," and he was right. It was a Scarborough bluff.

Despite a couple of dust-ups, I do love Chicago, and the people I worked with were very talented, very passionate, and very dedicated artists. The late Bernie Sahlins and the late Joyce Sloane were lovers of the arts, and generous believers in me. I am honoured to have had the privilege of walking that storied stage. Del Close was a creative genius, and amongst his talents was the gift of exploring and heightening the talents of others. He was a true revolutionary in the "Actors Liberation Movement," which is what Del liked to call improvisation. Above all, he was brave enough to insist on truth, even at the expense of a joke and even at his own expense.

He was a kingmaker, having honed the likes of Belushi and Farley, but he was so committed to the truth that he once bravely said of himself, "I am the door through which others pass, and I cannot." While he enjoyed comedy that came from a place of "wouldn't it be funny if . . . ," he treasured comedy of truth, comedy that started from, "isn't it funny that . . ." I owe much to Chicago, but I wasn't meant to stay there long.

Meanwhile, at that time, Toronto Second City was celebrating its fifteenth anniversary, and because I had moved to Chicago, I was now technically an alumnus, thus eligible to

199

participate in Toronto's star-studded fifteenth anniversary alumni show. Other alumni included Martin Short, Eugene Levy, Catherine O'Hara, Andrea Martin, Joe Flaherty, and Dave Thomas. In the crowd were many celebrities, like Michael Keaton, as well as producers and casting directors. It was a big deal. I flew back to Toronto and had the novel experience of staying in a hotel in my home city. When I got to the theatre, it was packed with television crews and fans waiting outside to see who was arriving. I, of course, took the subway there and entered through the back door because I was not somebody anyone wanted to see.

I went backstage, looked at the running order, and saw that I was in four sketches. Very few sketches compared to the star cast members. I was having feelings of not belonging. I got why the big stars were there, but I was unknown. During the first act, I did two of my four sketches. The first played to polite applause; the second was plagued with so much audience chatter that Michael Keaton generously began a shushing campaign. At the intermission, I went downstairs. I was despondent.

Dave Foley, from the Kids in the Hall, caught me downtrodden. He said, "What's going on? You're killing out there."

I said, "I feel like such an asshole. I shouldn't have come. The audience just wants to see the stars, and I don't blame them. I'm thinking of going home."

Then Foley said, "What do you have in the second act?"

I said, "I start the second act with Wayne Campbell."

He goes, "They're letting you do Wayne?! You're

I WAS IN VERY FEW SKETCHES COMPARED TO THE STAR CAST MEMBERS. I WAS HAVING FEELINGS OF NOT BELONGING.

Dave Foley. A Canadian genius.

gonna kill, asshole. It's gonna be great." It was the bucking up that I needed. Foley has always been my champion.

I changed into my Wayne costume and took my starting position, which happened to be in the crowd, breaking the fourth wall. The lights came up, drunken stragglers took their seats, and I began performing from the crowd. At first, people thought I was an underage heckler. Then, people started to get it. Then I got my first laugh. Then I took the stage. And then it started to grow. "B" laughs. Then "A" laughs. Then laughs where we had to hold, waiting for the audience to finish. Then everything played. And when the lights went out, there was thunderous applause, cheers, stomps, whistles. It was like a jet taking off. It had fucking killed. I was stunned.

There was an after-party upstairs, in the dining room above the theatre. As I took my place in the line, I heard a voice from below. It was Michael Keaton.

"Hey, kid." He ran up two flights of stairs. "That Wayne sketch is awesome. Congratulations!" I couldn't believe his generosity. My fellow linemates were just as blown away.

"That was Michael Keaton, you know."

"Oh, I know," I said.

At the after-party, there was a main table where all the big names, including the *SCTV* cast, sat and schmoozed. I took a table way in the corner, as far away from the main table as possible. The *SCTV* cast were and are my heroes, and I didn't want to crowd them, like others were doing. They came over and sat at my table. I couldn't believe it. They were so incredibly generous and nice. It was a magical evening.

The next day, I returned to Chicago and got a phone call. It was Lorne Michaels.

He offered me a job as a featured performer and writer on *Saturday Night Live*.

Martin Short had recommended me to Lorne, based on my performance at Toronto Second City's fifteenth anniversary show the night before. Another Canadian, Pam Thomas, producer on *The Kids in the Hall* and wife of Dave Thomas, who had also been there that night, also called Lorne on my behalf. Yet another Canadian, my dear friend Dave Foley, had called Lorne Michaels. I felt like I was being taken care of by the Canadian mob. I thank them all.

Many things coalesced on that day. I remembered that I had promised myself I would never go to New York unless I was offered a job. I flashed on the first time I saw *Saturday Night Live*, with Gilda Radner, when I, Sucky Baby, had precociously declared that I would someday be on that show. And I was also reminded that the person I most wanted to see me on *Saturday Night Live*, my dad, would never know.

When I got to New York City, it was a whole new world. Although Toronto is only five hundred miles away, it might as well have been in Alpha Centauri.

As a fellow Canadian, Lorne Michaels knew my particular challenges. He said I had a good chance of doing well at *SNL* because I would have the Canadian humility that says, "I'd better work hard and study." But he also cautioned that, as a Canadian, I would have a hard time accepting that talent and character don't always go hand in hand. He said that, as a Canadian, I would be devastated when one of my heroes turned out to be a prick. And of course, he was

right. Over time, I came to accept the talent–character discrepancy. But it's true.

Canadians will ask, "Have you met so-and-so?" and if I say yes, their follow-up question is, "Was so-and-so nice?"

Americans will ask, "Have you met so-and-so?" but their follow-up question is, "What's so-and-so like?"

Canadians need to know they were nice. Americans just want the inside scoop. If they're nice, fine. If not, oh well.

In many ways, because I was a fellow Canadian, Lorne took me under his wing. Lorne is very erudite,

203

Above: Lorne Michaels
and me in 2014. We are
backstage at *SNL*, moments
before I guest-performed
Dr. Evil in a sketch about
the controversial Seth Rogen
movie, *The Interview*. Seth
Rogen is from Vancouver.

———————————

Right: Louis Malle. To my
delight, Lorne invited me to
dinner with the great director.

with a wide knowledge of history and art and an appreciation of European films. I too loved European films, and because Toronto is such a movie town, I was familiar with many of the films he spoke about. I shared with Lorne my love of the French film director Louis Malle. To my delight, Lorne told me that not only was he friends with Louis Malle, but that in a few weeks he would be coming to New York because his wife, Candice Bergen, was going to be hosting *SNL*.

Lorne invited me to dinner with Malle. It was to be *My Dinner with Louis*. For the entire meal, I sat silent, intimidated by my boss and in awe of Monsieur Malle. Lorne told Louis that I had written a high school essay about his movie *Lacombe, Lucien*. The essay was called "Lucien Lacombe: Evil Villain or a Product of His Time?" Lorne, in an act of incredible generosity, said, "Mike, I believe you have a question for Louis."

I said, through a croaking voice, "Monsieur Malle, I wrote an essay about *Lacombe, Lucien*, in which I wondered if the main character, Lucien Lacombe, was evil or just a product of his time."

He said to me, "What conclusion did you draw?"

I said, "I thought he was a product of his time."

Louis Malle said, "Oh no, he was just evil." When does that ever happen in life? I felt like Woody Allen in *Annie Hall* being able to pull Marshall McLuhan from around the corner. People always say that you never use

Pauline Kael, The New Yorker:
A knockout. A major work. Malle succeeds triumphantly.
Vincent Canby, New York Times:
A beautifully considered, complex, disquieting film. You come out of the theatre so disturbed, you don't want to believe it.
Judith Crist, New York Magazine:
A remarkable work. It is the present perceived by an artist.

LACOMBE, LUCIEN
A FILM BY LOUIS MALLE

the knowledge you learned in high school. I beg to differ. Thank you, Canadian education system. And thank you, Lorne.

Lorne and I bonded over Canada. He was amused by my constant Canadian obsession with fairness— this wasn't fair, that wasn't fair. One day, somebody had done something to me that was absolutely, without question, so completely unfair. I was really upset, and, honestly, rightly so. In Scarborough, nobody likes a snitch, but this was so bad that I had to go and tell the boss. I waited an hour outside of Lorne's office, getting angrier and angrier at how unfair this person had been to me. By the time I got into his office, I was steaming.

IN SCARBOROUGH, NOBODY LIKES A SNITCH, BUT THIS WAS SO BAD THAT I HAD TO GO AND TELL THE BOSS.

I said, "Fuck me, Lorne. Blank blank did blank blank. That's so unfair."

Lorne said, "Yeah, you're right. But, Mike, you don't want the world to be fair."

I couldn't believe what I was hearing. Had so many years in New York erased every molecule of Lorne's Canadianness? I said, "What?! Of course we want the world to be fair."

Lorne said, "No, Mike. You don't want the world to be fair. For example, it's not fair that you're more talented than most people."

I was dumbstruck. What a brilliant way to get someone to get off the whole "fair" thing. Flattery! Genius! I don't know if Lorne actually believed the things he said about me, but I can tell you it stopped me cold. I could have slept for ten hours. I back-pocketed the "You don't want the world to be fair" move and have used it successfully with my children.

206

Lorne reminded me that I wasn't in Canada anymore. Here in America, people play for all the marbles. Americans pitied their athletes who only got a silver, feeling badly that the silver medallist had "lost." He said that the civility I had grown up with in Canadian show business was due to the fact that there was no money in it. It's very easy to be civil when the stakes are low. In America, the rewards were great, but so was the competition. And so was the pressure.

Working on *Saturday Night Live* is so all-pervasive that it's like working on a submarine under the polar ice cap. You write Monday and Tuesday, read the material Wednesday, rehearse Thursday, Friday, and during the day on Saturday, you do a dress rehearsal that isn't shown to the public, and then the actual show that airs live at 11:30 p.m., ending at 1 a.m. There's an obligatory party in Manhattan, and you get Sunday to nurse the hangover. And then it starts over again. The contract is for six years. Dana Carvey described being on the show as "once a week being shot out of a cannon with no net to catch you." Gilda Radner described *Saturday Night Live* as "an under-rehearsed Broadway opening once a week." She also said that "it's an insatiable monster that eats your material, insatiably." Lorne described the show as "the court of the Borgias, and even the nicest Borgia still has a poison ring."

On one occasion, a crew member gave me a cappuccino. Lorne took it out of my hands and said, "Do you know him?"

I said, "No."

"Never take a drink from someone you don't know." And he threw the coffee in the garbage.

And then, on my fourth show, I saw what he meant. I had been hired halfway through the season. I wasn't a full cast member, so I had to write for myself. I'd had some small pieces in sketches, but nothing I'd written had gotten into the show. As I mentioned before, Wednesday is read-through day. At read-through, the cast sits around a table with the host and Lorne, senior producers, and the director. Chairs are brought in that are arranged around the read-through table, forming a gallery. The writers all sat together on the right, production staff on the left, and the technical artisans in the centre. To call the read-through a tough room is like saying Ebola is a bad cold. The writers don't want you to succeed, the producers are afraid that the show's going to be too complicated to produce this week, and if you're a new guy, like I was, the technical staff don't know who you are and aren't sure you're going to be around next week. As for Lorne, the man has literally either heard, or written himself, every possible joke combination known to mankind.

It was Tuesday night. I had decided it was time to do my Wayne Campbell character on *SNL*. If it flamed out, I lost my big gun. I had struggled with how to introduce the character for the three previous shows, but I had hit on an idea of placing Wayne in a cable access show, as cable access was hitting its stride. I would make it the most local show in the history of television. It would literally be about Wayne's basement and, if he was feeling adventurous, upstairs. I struggled with having Wayne be a Canadian. I'd been in the States long enough to know that there was a universal, suburban, heavy metal kid experience:

the same long hair with baseball cap, workie boots, ripped jeans, black concert T-shirts, and the belief that Zep was God. And all heavy metal guys wanted to do was look for chicks.

And besides, within a week, I realized that none of my American coworkers, writers, or actors knew anything about Canada. Most thought that Montreal was the capital city, not Ottawa. The majority didn't realize that we had our own currency. They all thought that Canada only had winter. Some were confused that I was claiming to be Canadian, and yet I was only five-foot-seven, as if it was the land of giants.

So I started to play games.

I insisted that Canadian Tire money was our actual currency, a claim that went unchallenged. I told them that not only was there a Canadian Thanksgiving, but that there was a Canadian Christmas—in July, when Jesus actually died. That July, one sensitive American colleague sent me a Christmas card. I became a one-man public relations firm for Canada. I began to pretend that I wasn't familiar with universally known American customs. For example, I feigned ignorance of Independence Day, sarcastically asking if it was "America's equivalent of Canada Day." I pretended to not know the name of the World Series, coyly calling it the "Stanley Cup of baseball." Not only was I out of the country, but I was starting to go out of my mind. In retaliation, Kevin Nealon developed a "Mike Myers" impression that started every sentence with "In Canada . . . ," with the same singsong of the girl in *American Pie* who started every sentence with "This one time, at band camp . . ."

GREETINGS FROM AURORA, ONT.

I decided that Wayne would be from Aurora, Illinois, just outside of Chicago, because there is a town called Aurora, Ontario, just north of Toronto. Aurora, Ontario, is very similar to Scarborough. I made no concession to a Chicago accent. I wrote Wayne's first *SNL* sketch on a yellow legal pad, handwritten and stapled. I called the sketch "Wayne's World."

At five o'clock on Wednesday morning, I put the sketch on the hand-in pile outside the head writer's office. It was an intimidating pile, usually consisting of forty or so sketches. The cast and writers I had been hired into were

Let's Go... CANADA!

ISSUED BY THE DIRECTOR OF PUBLIC INFORMATION, UNDER THE AUTHORITY OF HON. J. T. THORSON, MINISTER OF NATIONAL WAR SERVICES, OTTAWA.   PRINTED IN CANADA — 22 - 1 L

of the highest quality. I thought they were going to be good; I didn't know they were going to be *that* good. I took a seat on one of the couches and started to drift off when one of the senior writers came into the read-through room, went over to the pile, and picked up my sketch. In my head, I was screaming, *You can't look at the pile!* But he was doing it. As he read my sketch, not only was he not laughing, but he was shaking his head in disgust. He caught me watching him.

He said to me, "Did you write this?"

Holding back both tears and vomit, I said, "Yes."

And with that, he took my sketch off the pile *and put it on the read-through table!*

My mind started racing. *What does that mean? Does it mean he just decided I wasn't allowed to hand it in? I didn't even know you were allowed to look at the pile. Wait a minute, he just took my sketch off the pile and put it on the read-through table.*

Then he left the room. I froze. A second later, another senior writer came in and picked up my sketch off the table and began to read it. His reaction was a little more animated. As he read, he said things like "No!" and "Oh my God, this sucks," and then "Seriously?"

He turned to me and said, "Don't hand this in. It sucks. You'll never win over the read-through table. Honestly, this sucks." Then he took my sketch *and threw it on the ground.* HE TOOK MY SKETCH AND THREW IT ON THE GROUND. It was five o'clock in the morning. I was jet-lagged. I was vomitous. I wasn't even angry, I was freaked out. I'd finally made it to *Saturday Night Live*, I had a character that people seemed to like in Canada, I thought I finally found a way to get it on the show, I'd worked my ass off combing through it over and over again, I'd gotten up the courage to put it on the dreaded pile, and now my career was over. I sat down for twenty minutes, staring into space, wondering what I was going to tell my friends in Toronto. I was trying to come up with what I call my "dignity answer," the story I would tell them about why I had been fired, while somehow making it seem it wasn't my fault and it was the best thing that had ever happened to me.

NOW MY CAREER WAS OVER. I SAT DOWN FOR TWENTY MINUTES, STARING INTO SPACE, WONDERING WHAT I WAS GOING TO TELL MY FRIENDS IN TORONTO.

And then something happened.

As if a hand had pulled me up by the scruff of my neck, I got up, went over to the sketch, restapled it, *and put it back on the pile.* I thought, *Fuck it. I'm not gonna let these assholes psych me out. If it dies at the read-through table, fair enough. But I'm going down swinging.*

A calmness came over me and I walked home through the empty, freezing canyons of Midtown to my four-hundred-square-foot apartment and slept. When I woke up at 1 p.m., I zipped in a cab to 30 Rock to see if my sketch had indeed been typed up and put into the read-through pack. It had, but it was sketch number 40 of forty sketches.

In order to soothe the host, the producers would front-load the read-through with sketches they thought were likely to get in. Best came first, worst came last. At around sketch number 20 in the running order, everyone starts to get antsy. They know that the crappy sketches are coming, everyone is sleep-deprived, and everyone starts to get hungry. Lorne starts to eat his carrots around now, which is tough because he reads the stage directions, so now, if your sketch is in the second half of the pack, the stage directions are read with a full mouth. Lorne himself sometimes would start to make comments about the quality of the second-half sketches, saying things like, "Honest to fuck, can't we screen some of this bullshit?" My sketch was last. The crowd's patience was running out.

Finally, it came to my sketch.

Lorne turned to everyone and said, "How are we all feeling? Should we do this?"

Dana shot a look over to me and gave me an encouraging thumbs-up. I piped up, "I think we should." Which, thankfully, got a smattering of chuckles. The sketch began. Lorne, now through a mouthful of popcorn, began the stage directions. I launched into the "Wayne's World" theme with every ounce of enthusiasm I could muster. Through sheer will, the song "'Wayne's World'! 'Wayne's World'! Party time! Excellent! *Erna erna-erna-erna wooooo!*" got a fairly significant laugh. Lorne's eyebrow raised.

And then our first joke got a good laugh. Then the next. Then we got a big woof. Then I did the theme again, and people were doing it along with me. Then another joke killed. And then it was over and it got a round of applause, which is a very rare thing at any time during the read-through. Even more rare when it's the last of forty sketches. Dana shot me another thumbs-up.

I mouthed "Thank you" to him because he didn't need to sell it as much as he did, but he sold the shit out of it. Which, because Dana was held in such high esteem, was the read-through equivalent of the *Good Housekeeping* Seal of Approval. People left the

read-through on a high. The technical staff gave me a pat on the back. The writers scattered. Phil Hartman put his arm around me and said, "I don't know if it's going to get in, but I think you may have won the table."

And then the wait began.

After read-through, there is a three-hour wait as you sit outside Lorne's office where you hope one of Lorne's assistants will come out of Lorne's office and call your name to have you come into the room. Lorne's assistants came in and out ten times; my name was not called. The show only ever mounted eleven to twelve sketches every week, so it wasn't looking good. I gathered my coat and made my way to the elevator bank, comforted by the fact that maybe Phil was right—that if it wasn't this week, it might be next week, but I certainly wasn't dead. I had just hit the elevator button when a frantic and angry assistant came up to me.

"Are you Mike Myers?"

"Yes," I said.

"Where the fuck are you going?" she demanded.

"Home," I said.

"Lorne wants you in there right now."

"Am I being fired?" I asked.

"No, asshole, your sketch, 'Wally's World,' is in. Better hustle. And next time, don't fucking make me look for you."

I ran to Lorne's office. The Canadian comedian Leslie Nielsen was the host. Lorne sat at his desk, the Empire State Building behind his head. The producers

sat in their chairs against the wall. From the look of it, "Wayne's World" was not their first choice. Lorne said to me, "You got called ten minutes ago. Stay close. Here's the deal: it's in, but it's last. If the show runs over, it'll get cut. Is there a way to work Leslie into it?"

For some stupid reason, I said, "No."

Lorne said, "'Yes' is a better answer."

"Oh, okay."

"Do you know what to do?"

"No," I said.

Lorne said, "Go ask a grown-up. And don't ever make me wait again."

I walked out of the office. I say "I walked out of the office," but I don't remember actually moving my legs. I wanted to cry from relief, but I always remember what my dad said whenever I scored a goal. He would say, "After it goes in, casually walk back to your position as if it's no big deal and it happens all the time." Although my dad was still alive, his Alzheimer's had taken away much of his personality. I had never missed my dad more than at that moment, and I couldn't help but feel that it was his hand that lifted me up by the scruff and made me put the sketch back on the pile.

Conan O'Brien came to my aid. He saw my stunned look and said to me, "That 'Wayne's World' thing is so fuckin' funny, and so fuckin' weird. The song—it's so stupid. Do you know what to do?"

"No," I said.

He said, "Follow me."

He took me into a room that I didn't know existed, because I'd never had a sketch get on before. Just to the left of Lorne's office was a whole other office where the sets were designed, the costumes were put together, and where the floor director—the wonderful, patient,

caring, sensitive, but nobody's fool, Kenny Aymong—
had his lair. Kenny would tell you where your sketch
was in the running order, what stage your sketch would
be on in Studio 8H, what time on Thursday your sketch
would be rehearsed, and then he would lead you
through the process of rewrites and, most important,
how you got your sketch onto the cue cards. Kenny
took me under his arm for the whole six years I was
there. In fact, the entire crew took me under their arms.
I love those people.

I survived the week of rehearsal. Every week, Lorne
mounts roughly twelve sketches, and only ten make it.
There are two shows on Saturday night: the first show,
called the dress show, which is an 8:30 p.m. dress
rehearsal, and then the air show, which is the main
broadcast at 11:30 p.m. During the dress show,
"Wayne's World" was on last. Sketches on last have a
hard time making it to the air show. Audiences are
tired by then.

Our performance during the dress show felt like it
went well.

And then the waiting began. Would our sketch
make it to air?

Lorne has another office on the ninth floor that
overlooks the eighth-floor studio. It is tiny. When you
have a sketch that might make the show, you wait in a
room next to it. When Lorne has picked the air show,
an assistant opens the door and you're let in.

The door opened and immediately I looked to the
running order, which is on the big board at the far end
of the room. For each sketch, there's a 3 x 5 card, and all
the 3 x 5 cards are in the show order. To the left of the
big board is where the 3 x 5 cards of sketches that

217

didn't make it are pinned willy-nilly. I looked to the left. *Phew.* We were in.

I looked for my sketch. Once again, "Wayne's World" was the last sketch of the show, but we were in. Or were we?

Lorne went through the notes. The notes are often brutal and remarkably detailed. Things like clocks being the wrong time, maps being out of date, jokes that didn't work, minutes that need to be taken out, etc. When he got to "Wayne's World," he had a few notes, one of which was that he didn't want me to push it too much, and then he said, "Be prepared. If

we run over, 'Wayne's World' is cut." Then we had to rush to the assistants and give them the cuts and changes, and then you have to rush to the cue cards to give them the cuts and changes, and then you run over the cue cards to make sure that things are spaced right. Then you run to makeup. And then it's show time. I was blown away, and continue to be blown away, every time the late Don Pardo said my name. Such history.

The show progressed. Sketches that killed at read-through and were flat in dress were killing on the air show. Sketches that were okay at read-through and had killed at dress were a little flat on air. I was astonished at how unpredictable the success of a sketch was. Halfway through the show, "Wayne's World" had still not been cut. Three-quarters of the way through, still not cut. Four-fifths of the way through, I got summoned to Lorne's third office, which is under the bleachers.

Lorne said, "If this next sketch goes long and the musical act goes long, you're cut."

I sat beside him. The sketch ran short. And the musical act was perfectly on time.

Lorne turned to me and, in a scene that seemed to be taken from a movie, said, "All right, you're on."

I was pumped. And by now, calm. Just ready to enjoy it. We went out there, the sketch started, it played okay at first, and then we got our first big laugh. Then another. And a nice round of applause at the end.

I went onstage for the goodnights. I was emotionally exhausted but unbelievably proud. I had only one day to recover, and then it would all start again.

219

When Dave Foley heard that I had been hired for *SNL*, he told me to hang out with Phil Hartman. Foley said that Phil was my type of performer: he did characters, he had fantastic concentration, and he always tried his hardest, even if the material wasn't strong. More important, Foley told me that Phil was from Canada—Brantford, Ontario, to be precise, the home of Wayne Gretzky. Phil had been on the show for three years before I got hired, and I had never seen him perform, because I was living in England. When I was briefly living in Toronto, I worked Saturday nights at Second City, and I had one of those early, Soviet, top-loading VCRs that only gave you three and a half hours of tape. Being a die-hard Leafs fan, on Saturday I had to choose between taping the game or *Saturday Night Live*. I'll let you guess which program got taped. As a sidebar, because of my VCR situation, I never saw Dana's Church Lady or Jon Lovitz's Liar until I was on the show. I did watch Gary Leeman of the Toronto Maple Leafs score thirty goals that year. Further sidebar: my best friend, Dave Mackenzie, played on Gary Leeman's soccer team for a while. But I digress.

As luck would have it, I was seated next to Phil at the read-through table, and in my first week I struck up a conversation with him, launching headlong into Leafs banter. Phil was not a hockey fan. In fact, Phil had moved to America at the age of ten, and while he had great affection for Canada, he had only a cursory knowledge of it. With that first meeting, a running gag was born, wherein I insisted that he was the most Canadian person I'd ever met. And in some ways, it was true. Phil was a true team player. He was studious; he did his homework. On read-through day, he was the first to the table to study his stack of sketches, which was half a foot tall (my stack, for comparison, was an inch tall). Phil would insert the sketches into his official *Saturday Night Live* binder, which you're given when you join the cast, which nobody except

Phil used. Moreover, Phil customized his *SNL* binder with a three-holed, zippered, see-through binder sleeve that contained coloured pencils, erasers, Post-Its, and mints.

Phil Hartman's instrument, his body and his voice, was so versatile and refined that I have never seen anything like it, except perhaps for Peter Sellers or Dan Aykroyd. Before the read-through, Phil went through each sketch and made coded margin notes. Phil had determined that he had eleven "core characters," each of whom was numbered. For example, his Charlton Heston voice was a core character, and it was designated as number 3. If a number 3 was an authority figure, a blue pencil mark was put next to it. If it was an angry number 3 authority figure, a red pencil mark would go next to the blue pencil mark. The intensity of any character was measured on a scale out of ten, and in green pencil he would designate the correct intensity to the right of the colour designates. In summation, if the character kind of talked like Charlton Heston and was an angry authority figure who was mildly intense, Phil would make the following notation:

$$3 \mid \mid 6$$

He had created for himself the comedy character equivalent of musical notation. You can't get more Canadian than that. We love our standardized units of weights and measurements.

Phil could make anything funny, which, of course, was why everyone wrote for him, including me. Phil could save not only a sketch, but an entire show. He held the show together. After any sketch where Phil

knocked it out of the park, it became customary for the entire read-through table and audience to go, "Gluuuuue."

And it was my job to be the "sports announcer" who went, "They're not saying 'boo,' folks, they're saying 'glue.' Another fine performance from Mr. Phil Hartman of Brantford, Ontario."

After a while, Phil didn't write sketches. He didn't have to. I, of course, always had to write sketches. Tuesday night was writing night, and my office was next to Phil's. While I spent the entire evening pulling out my hair trying to come up with an idea, Phil was relaxed and sat at his desk doing various hobbies. One day, I passed his office and he said, "Kid, come in. Do you have any interest in diamonds?" He had a jeweller's loupe on his eye, and he was looking at some diamonds he had just bought. "Mike, when buying diamonds, you have to examine each stone for the four Cs: cut, carat, colour, and clarity." I assured Phil that I wasn't going to be buying diamonds anytime soon. In fact, if I didn't come up with a sketch that night, the only thing I'd be buying would be a one-way ticket back to Toronto.

On another Tuesday writing night, Phil was once again in his office, this time looking at helicopter shots of vacation property in the British Virgin Islands.

"Mike, come on in, kid," he said. "The three most important things in real estate are location, location, and location."

"Thanks, Phil," I said.

My favourite Tuesday night was one time when I popped into his office to say hello, only to be told, "Shh! Don't move." Phil was sweating, and he was staring intently at something on his desk through a high-powered magnifying glass attached to a flexy arm. I approached gingerly. Phil was using special long tweezers and special long scissors. And then it occurred to me, Phil was putting a ship in a bottle. I had walked in on him at the critical moment where one pulls the string that lifts the mainsail. With the steady hand of a surgeon, Phil calmly used the tweezers to tie off the mainsail string, and then he snipped off the remainder of the string using the special long scissors. I, however, was a nervous wreck, so hopped up on coffee that I could barely hold a pencil, and here was Phil, putting a ship into a bottle.

I said, "A ship in a bottle?"

"Mikey, you need to get a hobby," he said.

PHIL HAD SEVERAL HIGH-QUALITY, GLOSSY BROCHURES DISPLAYING FIREARMS. HE WAS PLANNING TO BUY A GUN.

Unfortunately, the last time I passed his office on a writing night was the most disturbing. Phil had several high-quality, glossy brochures displaying firearms. He was planning to buy a gun.

"Mikey, come on in," he said. "Have you ever thought about buying a gun?"

"I'm Canadian, Phil." I'd never seen a gun brochure before. It looked illicit, like weird porn—freaky-deeky Danish porn where "things" are put into "things." I didn't want to look at them. I said to him, "Phil, you're not going to buy a fucking gun, are you?"

"It's a dangerous world out there, Mikey," he said.

"Are you aware of the statistics of people being killed by their own guns? And besides, Phil, you're a Canadian."

Phil said, "I live in the Valley, Mikey. Have you seen the statistics of the police response times?"

I left his office with an uneasy feeling.

On a happier note, one of the greatest moments of my time on *Saturday Night Live* was when Wayne Gretzky was the host! I immediately called my friends in Toronto. I thought I was being punked, and as luck would have it, Wayne was going to be on "Wayne." I wrote a fantasy scene into the sketch, just so I could play hockey with Wayne Gretzky. Gretzky is not only the Great One, but he was one of *Saturday Night Live*'s best hosts. He was a true gentleman. And at the end of the week, he gave me a game-used Wayne Gretzky hockey stick: a Titan TPM 2020 with his patented gripper butt end. It even had the talcum powder left on the tape-wrapped blade. Inscribed on it was TO MIKE, THANKS FOR ALL THE FUN AT SNL. YOUR FRIEND (I THANK YOU), WAYNE GRETZKY. It is still one of my most prized possessions. It's my Excalibur.

———

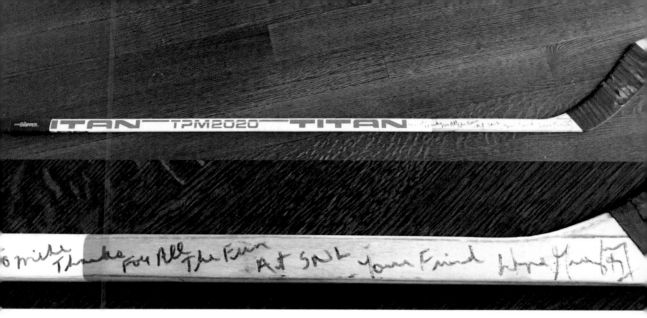

Four months later, on the day of the last show of the season, my first season, I came to 30 Rock and was approached by a journalist.

"Mr. Myers, what are your thoughts about Gilda Radner?" he asked.

I thought, *That's weird. How did they know that Gilda Radner had played my mum in a TV commercial in Canada?*

I said, "What do you mean?"

The reporter said, "Gilda Radner died this morning."

I felt like somebody had punched me in the gut. It seemed so strange that, just as I was hitting a bit of a stride on the show, the lady I had fallen in love with as a little kid, whom I admired on the show, and the original cast member I ultimately felt I was most similar to, had died that day. I went to my office and cried. I didn't care if somebody called me Sucky Baby.

After that show, which was the season finale, the mood was sombre. The after-party was subdued, but because tradition dictates that it take place outdoors in Rockefeller Plaza, where the hockey rink is during the winter months, I could see leaves budding on the trees that surround the piazza. It felt like a rebirth. The senior writer who had implored me not to hand in "Wayne's World" glanced my way sheepishly from across the way. He came over.

"Mike?"

"What?"

"Um, can I ask you a favour?"

"What?"

"My little brother wants to meet you . . . He's a big fan."

There was something about it being spring, and about Gilda's passing that day, that allowed me to drop my armour.

I said enthusiastically, "Of course!"

The writer's brother came over. He was fourteen years old and very starstruck. He said, "Mr. Myers, I'm your biggest fan. I love 'Wayne's World.' It's my favourite sketch!"

I said, "Thank you. But you know that I'm your brother's biggest fan. He's a genius. I learn from him every week." I saw the face of the fourteen-year-old brother brighten with pride for his older brother. The writer, who had been so offensive when I first joined the show, was puzzled at first, and then disarmed. I had seen how hard it had been for him to ask me, his "enemy," to meet his brother. It was an act of humble generosity for his brother, and ultimately, I saw it as a bid for connection, or at the very least, the opportunity to make amends.

I hate fighting. Although you can't tell from hockey, Canadians don't like fighting. We'll fight if we have to. I also hate grudges. My dad used to say that there was a condition known as "Liverpool Alzheimer's," where you forget everything except the grudges. And of course,

I was reminded that my father had actual Alzheimer's, and in remembering that, I realized that life is short, and sometimes people don't know how to be. Myself included.

In 1990, Lorne Michaels asked me if I wanted to make a movie, and we both agreed that "Wayne's World," the sketch, could be *Wayne's World*, the movie. I think this is a good time to make a definitive statement: Wayne Campbell is a Canadian character. There, I said it.

I mean, who are we kidding? Let's look at the name: Wayne. That is one of the most Canadian names ever, notwithstanding the obvious Wayne Gretzky. Wayne's last name, Campbell. So many Canadians have Scottish last names. Garth is also a Canadian name. Wayne was a Canadian name of my generation, and Garth of a previous generation. Wayne plays street hockey and says, "Car!" when a car comes and "Game on!" when it has passed. Wayne goes to Stan Mikita's Donuts, which is a thinly veiled reference to Tim Hortons. The cop at Stan Mikita's Donuts is named Officer Koharski, which refers to an incident that happened on *Hockey Night in Canada* when New Jersey Devils coach Jim Schoenfeld shouted at referee Don Koharski, on national TV, "Have another doughnut, you fat pig!" I was determined to inject elements of my Canadian childhood into the movies I was making in the States, to prove that my formative years in Canada weren't just a dream. I call them "letters to Canada." Therefore, in a letter to Canada, the officer was named Koharski, and he was at a doughnut shop.

Aurora is Aurora—that's easy. The bar where Wayne meets Cassandra, played by Tia Carrere, is called the Gasworks. The Gasworks was a heavy

metal bar on Yonge Street in Toronto. Most notably, to myself, the Gasworks was a place that sold Molson Canadian lager in the big "quart" bottles—danger! The production designer on *Wayne's World* was a Canadian named Gregg Fonseca. Not only did he know the Gasworks, but he also came up with the idea of putting the one-storey-high, rotating table hockey player depiction of Stan Mikita on the roof of Stan Mikita's Donuts. In an example of life imitating art, there is a one-storey-high, rotating table hockey depiction of Wayne Gretzky on top of his restaurant in Toronto.

While some of the filmmaking team wanted the theme music under the opening credits to be a current Guns N' Roses song, I wanted it to be a Queen song. The iconically English band Queen was huge when I was growing up in Canada. Even the Mirthmobile— Wayne's car, the second-hand, powder blue AMC Pacer—seems somehow Canadian. Again, other members of the filmmaking team wondered why Wayne wouldn't have a "cool" car.

But the most obvious proof that Wayne is a Canadian character is that he speaks with a Canadian accent! He speaks like everybody I knew growing up in Scarborough.

Even after *Wayne's World*, I tried to write "letters to Canada" into my movies. In *Austin Powers*, Mindy Sterling's character—Frau Farbissina, Dr. Evil's wife— is a mélange of Rosa Klebb, the villain in the 1967 James Bond film *From Russia with Love*, and Lotta Hitschmanova. Lotta Hitschmanova was the head of the

Dr. Brian May ✔
@DrBrianMay

I'd forgotten how great this is. Respects to Mike Myers ! Bri X

Lilybop @lilybop2010

Mike Myers & crew tell the inside story of the 'Wayne's World' 'Bohemian Rhapsody' Scene @adamlambert @DrBrianMay rollingstone.com/music/news/the...

charitable organization known as the Unitarian Service Committee of Canada (USCC). She has often been called the Mother Teresa of Canada. I came to know her through the low-budget, late-night commercials for the USCC, in which she implored Canadians to give generously to the world's poor. She spoke with a Dracula accent (she pronounced *Ottawa* as "Ottava") and wore a self-made paramilitary uniform. She scared the shit out of me. Was she in the army? Was she in her own army? Why did she talk like a vampire? This inspired me to say of Frau Farbissina that she was in the militant wing of the Salvation Army.

Also, Lotta Hitschmanova spoke and dressed like the terrifying, Russian, confirmed bachelorette Rosa Klebb whose weapon of choice was a shoe knife. On top of if all, the name of the actress who played Rosa Klebb was Lotte Lenya. Lotta's first name also inspired Alotta Fagina, the gun moll of Robert Wagner's cycloptic character, Number 2. It was also an homage to the Bond villainess Pussy Galore.

The name Dr. Evil came from a headline from the British tabloid, *The Sun*. My brother Peter had taken a photograph of the headline of *The Sun*, which read SEX SLAVES OF DR. EVIL. In the scene where Dr. Evil and Scott Evil are in group therapy with Carrie Fisher, the first father and son to "share" are named Mr. Keon and his son, Dave. Dave Keon, of course, is my favourite Toronto Maple Leaf. In *Austin 1*, my United Nations Security Council included Canada, with our representative dressed as a Mountie. In *Austin 2*, a news ticker reads LEAFS WIN THE STANLEY CUP and TORONTO VOTED BEST CITY IN THE WORLD. The song that Heather Graham's character, Felicity

Shagwell, danced to was "American Woman," by Winnipeg's own, the Guess Who.

At a certain point, after I'd lived in the States for a while, a crisis of Canadian identity began to consume me. There was no CBC; people didn't know or care about Canada. I had Canadian friends, but they were few and far between, and we clung to each other unhealthily. But there was a different complication subsuming my Canadian identity: I had become famous. I was a public person. And as I mentioned at the beginning of this book, Canada is not a famous country, it distrusts fame, and nothing about a Canadian childhood teaches you how to circumnavigate the snakes and ladders of a public life. With my newfound celebrity, I was having an out-of-body experience—and what's worse is that I was out of body and out of country. But moreover, when it came to Canada, I was out of touch.

And what happened next put me out of commission . . .

PART THREE

Love

CHAPTER FIVE

Losing Canada

O N NOVEMBER 21, 1991,
I was in my apartment in New York City after finishing
a read-through at *Saturday Night Live*. I got a call from
my mother in Toronto that my father's Alzheimer's had
progressed to the point where parts of his body were
shutting down. He wasn't going to make it through
the night. My mum said I should wait by the phone
for updates.

I had written a sketch that had gotten into that
week's show, with a recurring character named Simon,
a little English boy with no mother, the mother being
"with the angels." Simon was a pastiche of every one
of my English cousins, who had insanely charming
English accents, unlike the horrific Canadian accent
that had so offended my father's sensibilities. In many

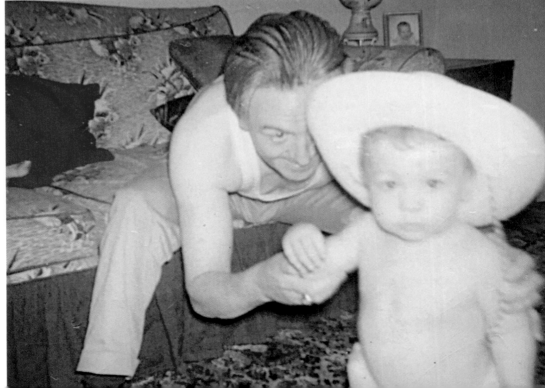

ways, I created Simon, the little English boy, to prove to my dad that, if I wanted, I could be an English child and please him. So much of my career was about pleasing him—not in a bid for acceptance, because I always had his acceptance, but in a bid to honour him.

I put on the Beatles song "Across the Universe," partly out of homage to my father's Liverpool roots, and partly because that song, to me, is a perfect piece of art. The song makes you *feel* like you are travelling across the universe.

I fell asleep in my chair, only to be awakened by the telephone. The same phone that, over the years, had consistently given me fantastic news about my career and, with equal consistency, had given me horrific news about my father's health. It was my mum. He was gone.

I was numb.

There are moments in life when you ask yourself, "How did I get here?"

Earlier that summer, I had finished shooting my first movie, *Wayne's World*. I would say that it was a great disappointment that he died before my first film was released, but in fact, the greater disappointment was that he had gotten sick the second my career had started to take off, and he had seen nothing of my success on *Saturday Night Live*. The finality that I would never be able to share any of this with him set in. As I sat alone at my desk, the proverbial big chill overcame me.

And yet, strangely, I was relieved.

Alzheimer's is a horrible disease, and by the end you just want it over.

My mum called back and insisted that I do the show that Saturday. "The show must go on, Michael."

237

I then called my best friend, Dave Mackenzie. He was devastated. He had loved my father, and my dad had loved Mackenzie as if he were his own son. I found myself taking care of Mackenzie, because that guy can go morbid, in true Canadian fashion.

I called Lorne. He was fantastic, as Lorne always is in these moments. He asked me if I had spoken to my mother, and I relayed to him that my mum wanted me to do the show that Saturday. Lorne agreed. "The show must go on, Mike."

MY MUM INSISTED THAT I DO THE SHOW THAT SATURDAY. "THE SHOW MUST GO ON, MICHAEL."

I flew up to Toronto. It was one of those sunny but freezing Toronto days. I took a cab out to Scarborough, to the funeral home. In the cab, I got recognized, and it was very weird to be a famous person in Canada, but it was equally weird to be a famous person at such a personal time. It was very confusing. For all of my life in Canada, especially out in Scarborough, I was just a private citizen, and in some irrational way I thought, *Don't these people know what just happened?* Even on the most basic level, I couldn't understand how people on the street were smiling and going on with their day.

When I got to the funeral home, my brothers and Mackenzie were there. We went down to the basement to pick out a casket. I thought to myself, *All right, Mackenzie, here we are, picking out my dad's casket, in the middle of Scarborough. Surely to God, you can't get more morbid than this.* We selected a casket, and the uncomfortable but necessary conversation of casket pricing began. Mackenzie, out of respect, took a walk around the showroom. When the business was concluded, Mackenzie came back, stricken. White as a ghost.

I said, "Mackenzie, what's wrong?"

Zombie-like, he pointed to the corner. "Baby coffins, eh?"

In the corner, there were, indeed, small coffins.

He said it again, "Baby coffins . . . For kids, eh?"

I thought, *Holy crap, Mackenzie. Just when I thought you couldn't get more morbid than picking out my father's casket, you manage to up your morbidity game by feeling it necessary for me to see the baby coffins. Well played, Mackenzie. Well played, Canada.*

After the funeral, I went to my mum's house. She gave me some of my father's items: his *Encyclopaedia Britannica* ring, his Royal Engineers cap badge, and, surprisingly, his Canadian citizenship papers. I had no idea he had become a Canadian citizen.

That Saturday on the show, I did the Simon sketch, the sketch about the little English boy in the bath whose "mummy is with the angels." My heart was ripped out of my chest. I didn't know whether I was

going to be able to finish it. After the sketch, I put on my street clothes and found a quiet part of Studio 8H and cried. A deep cry. From across the universe.

I was changed.

I was heartbroken, demoralized, spiritually rudderless. My dad's death had rocked my world. I had gone up to Canada almost every weekend while I was on *Saturday Night Live* to visit him. And now, the thought of going up to a fatherless Canada became torturous. I knew every

239

square inch of Toronto. If friends said, "Meet me at Queen and Spadina," and I was at College and McCaul, I wouldn't need a map, I wouldn't even need to know what street I was walking on—my feet would just take me there. And on the way, signposts from my life, mental Google pins, would pop up every twenty feet. *There's where I met my first girlfriend. There's where I saw Max Webster.* And then, after my father's death it became, *There's where my dad took me to Shopsy's Deli to get a corned beef sandwich.* And *There's where my dad used to work.* And *There's where my dad used to park the car when we went to the CNE.* And so on and so on.

Several years before my father's death, I bought a cottage north of Toronto. It had several acres of woods, with a spring-fed pond that, during the winter, froze flat, making a rink of dreams. I made a little changing shelter, strung up some lights, and skated and stickhandled in the delicious quiet that the snow-laden trees had created. This was my Canadian dream. I rarely left the house, opting instead to just take in nature, hiking, making trails.

I went to an IGA supermarket in Coboconk, Ontario. While trying to buy Kraft Macaroni and Cheese—which we in Canada call Kraft Dinner—a stock boy was pricing cans of Puritan Irish Stew and stopped abruptly when he recognized me. He dropped his price gun and zombie-walked away, as if he had seen a g-g-g-ghost. Ten seconds later, I heard over the PA, "Ladies and gentlemen, Canada's own Mike Myers is in aisle 4." I was surrounded by two hundred people. The store manager handed me a wireless microphone. My impromptu speech began: "People of IGA, I'm not one for speechifying, but the hospitality you have shown me here in aisle 4 has left an indelible mark on my heart." I posed for a few pictures—not many, as these were the days before cell phone cameras—but in the melee, I never did get my Kraft Dinner. Instead I made a beeline to the car.

In the netherworld between the two sets of automatic doors was a bank of coin-operated vending machines. One of the machines was *Wayne's World* themed, but it was clear that it was not officially licensed. It seemed foreign. The cardboard insert looked photocopied and the *Wayne's World* logo wasn't quite right. Inside the machine, they sold those plastic bubbles, each containing a button with a catchphrase from *Wayne's World* printed on it. Two of the buttons caught my eye. One said, "Scwing!" which I realized was probably supposed to be "Schwing!" and the other one said, "Half Blown Clinks." Half blown clinks? Wayne never said "Half blown clinks." I bought them both, of course.

When I got to the car, I realized that these buttons were indeed foreign knockoffs and that "Half blown clinks" was probably "I've blown chunks." It was literally a case of Broken Telephone or, as the English call that game, Chinese Whispers. It was getting surreal.

Another day when I was at my cottage, I went into Haliburton, a charming Canadian town north of Toronto, famous for McKeck's Tap & Grill, owned by former Toronto Maple Leaf Walt McKechnie.

Outside McKeck's, a dude came up to me and said, "Mike Myers?"

"That's me!" I said.

"Mike Myers. What are you doing . . . *here*?"

"I used to come to Haliburton as a kid."

Then he said, "Yeah, but what are you doing here . . . *now*? You could be *anywhere*."

And then he walked away laughing, the assumption being that, despite my recent success, I was perhaps too dumb to know that there were other places in the world to go to, like Paris or Berlin or Thailand.

It made me sad. Why not Haliburton? I like Haliburton. I thought of John Candy at the Toronto airport.

Between my father's death and encounters like this, trips to Canada became more painful, and thus became less frequent, until, for many years, I would only come up for Christmas.

TRIPS TO CANADA **BECAME** MORE **PAINFUL, AND THUS BECAME** LESS FREQUENT.

I was getting busier. Movies, TV shows, books, promotional tours. More promotional tours. Writing, more writing. Writing while on promotional tours. It was a thrilling time. A confusing time. A gratifying time that I am extremely grateful for, but it left very little time to come home. But home was changing.

Canada, for me, was a place that I knew intimately from 1963 until 1983, when I moved to England. It was my sanctuary. It's where I had lived as a private person, as an observer. But now, as a public person in Canada, I had become the observed. Not all attention is flattering, and in aggregate, constant attention can quickly turn into scrutiny, and scrutiny is not always fun and not always comfortable. In my youth, I would absorb Canadian life like a sponge, effortlessly, joyfully, unselfconsciously. Then one day, casual observations became political statements. Going to the hockey game became a public appearance instead of just watching the Leafs. Riding the subway, my beloved TTC, was called, by some cynics, an attempt to appear to be a "man of the people," or even less

It really is the better way.

generously, to "get recognized." I can tell you that it was just an attempt to get to my destination, and if there was a secondary motivation in taking the "Red Rocket," it was an attempt to get a deep hit of Canada. A super-toke of home. A fix of the familiar. I knew what was happening, but I couldn't stop it.

I was losing Canada.

And Canada was losing Canada.

The Canada I know was disappearing. Electrohome, the Canadian company that made televisions, the same televisions that I watched Team Canada beat the Soviet Union on, went out of business. As did Clairtone, the Canadian company that made our record player. Lowney's candies, makers of the Cherry Blossom, were bought by the American company Hershey. Eaton's department store and catalogue business went belly-up. The Eaton's catalogue was as much a part of the Canadian experience as Macy's and the Thanksgiving Day Parade are for America. The landmark Toronto heavy metal bar, the Gasworks, which I paid homage to in *Wayne's World*, closed in 1993.

In 1999, the Leafs moved from Maple Leaf Gardens to the Air Canada Centre. I took this hard. Perhaps, in an irrational way, I took it personally.

These are the ticket stubs of the last three games that I saw the Maple Leafs play at Maple Leaf Gardens.

SEC.	ROW	SEAT
47	G	15

E A S T

Retain Stub — Good Only
(12)
SAT.
8:00 P.M. **Nov. 3**
Davis Printing Limited 1990
CALGARY FLAMES
VS.
TORONTO MAPLE LEAFS
ADMIT ONE. Entrance by Main Door or by Church Street Door.

SEC.	ROW	SEAT
48	M	10

W E S T

Retain Stub — Good Only
(19)
MON.
7:30 P.M. **Nov. 19**
Davis Printing Limited 1990
BOSTON BRUINS
VS.
TORONTO MAPLE LEAFS
ADMIT ONE. Entrance by Main Door or by West Door, Carlton St.

SEC.	ROW	SEAT
77	M	10

E A S T

Retain Stub — Good Only
(20)
SAT.
8:00 P.M. **Nov. 24**
Davis Printing Limited 1990
EDMONTON OILERS
VS.
TORONTO MAPLE LEAFS
ADMIT ONE. Entrance by Main Door or by Church Street Door.

MATTAMY ATHLETIC CENTRE

MAPLE LEAF GARDENS

243

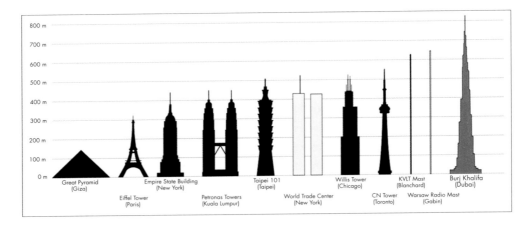

800 m
700 m
600 m
500 m
400 m
300 m
200 m
100 m
0 m

Great Pyramid (Giza)   Eiffel Tower (Paris)   Empire State Building (New York)   Petronas Towers (Kuala Lumpur)   Taipei 101 (Taipei)   World Trade Center (New York)   Willis Tower (Chicago)   CN Tower (Toronto)   KVLT Mast (Blanchard)   Warsaw Radio Mast (Gabin)   Burj Khalifa (Dubai)

In 2004, the Montreal Expos moved to Washington, D.C., becoming the Washington Nationals. It's as if every last trace of Expo 67 was being "unpersoned," expunged from the national consciousness. In 2007, the CN Tower was no longer the tallest freestanding structure in the world. It was usurped by the Burj Khalifa in Dubai without any outrage, disappointment, or attempt to right the wrong. Canada didn't have the fire in its belly to compete with cities like

Dubai, as it had in 1973 when the tower was built. Even BlackBerry, that lone Canadian success story, failed to keep up with the competition, and from 2013 to 2014, its number of users worldwide dropped from 85 million to 46 million. My Canada was dying.

Al Waxman from *King of Kensington* died in 2001. So did Ernie Coombs, Mr. Dressup. Glenn Cochrane from CFTO-TV News passed away in 2012, but wherever he goes in heaven, I'm sure he's never too far from a coupla lovely ladies. In 2007,

Sam the Record Man closed its doors. (Its founder, Sam Sniderman, died five years later, at the age of ninety-two.)

In 2013, the CBC lost *Hockey Night in Canada*. There still is a *Hockey Night in Canada*, and for a few years it will air on the CBC too, but it's not the same. It should just be on the CBC. And as if that weren't bad enough, in 2008 *Hockey Night in Canada* lost the rights to the *Hockey Night in Canada* theme song! Come on, people, it's *Hockey Night in Canada*, for God's sakes.

The question of whether Canada would stay together as a contiguous nation was still unresolved, and throughout the nineties, I watched from America as Quebec had endless debates on the separatism issue, causing a drip, drip, drip of national anxiety. Things nearly reached a breaking point in 1995, when Quebec voted to stay in Canada by a margin of one percentage point. We could've had a Quebexit. But one part of Canada did actually separate.

My friend Rob Cohen in a men's room in Calgary. This is a mirror inside the bathroom where you measure yourself against the height of famous Canadians. I was not the shortest. Phew.

In 1999, a new territory, one with a primarily Aboriginal population, was created near the Arctic Circle. Its name? Nunavut. When my brother told me that it was called Nunavut, I thought he was joking, because it sounded like he was saying that "the Inuit didn't want to be part of Canada anymore—'none of it.'"

"None of what?" I said. "They're not getting anything?"

"No, the Inuit are getting 'none of it.'"

"For God's sakes, can't they have some of it and we'll call it a day?"

My brother said, "They are getting some of it! None of it!"

But unlike Abbott and Costello, my brother stopped the conversation and said, "Oh, you think I'm saying 'none of it.' The new aboriginal territory is called N-U-N-A-V-U-T. Nunavut." Who's on First Nations?

There were some Canadian cultural success stories. The Canadarm was developed for the American space shuttle program. Designed in Canada, the Canadarm was how the space shuttle retrieved satellites. The word CANADA was printed along the length of the Canadarm in oversized letters. I'm not going to pooh-pooh the technological achievements of this engineering marvel; I will leave that to my American friends who hold me personally accountable for what they deem to be a modest achievement. Personally, the Canadarm and its oversized logo remind me of my childhood, when I would write C A N A D A on the side of my Airfix Saturn V model rocket.

Even though I wasn't going up to Canada as frequently as I had before my father's death, Canada still dominated my consciousness while I was living in the States. There's no one more Canadian than a Canadian who no longer lives in Canada.

While living in Los Angeles, I communed with my Canadianness by playing hockey twice a week. Ironically,

246

EXPLORE CANADA'S ARCTIC

10858N

NUNAVUT

08 09 05 06

I was playing more hockey on ice in Los Angeles than I ever had during my childhood in Canada.

I was in Paris when the Leafs got to the Stanley Cup semifinals in 1993. Because of the time difference, I awoke to the tragic news that Wayne Gretzky had knocked the Leafs out of the playoffs. I was the only person in Paris who was crying not because of how beautiful the City of Lights is, but because this was the closest the Leafs had come to a Stanley Cup since 1967.

During the 2002 Winter Olympics at Salt Lake City, I was thrilled Team Canada won the gold medal in men's hockey, beating the U.S., 5–2. I watched the game in L.A. with a Canadian writer-director friend of mine, Calgary's own Rob Cohen. When Canada won, we got into a car and drove around Beverly Hills with a Canadian flag streaming out the window, honking the horn incessantly, in hopes of sharing the celebration with fellow Canucks. No one honked back. In desperation, we drove to the Roots clothing store in Beverly Hills. Roots is a Canadian company, and we

This is me in Calgary taking
penalty shots on Tretiak. He
let me score. Class act.

assumed that fellow Canadians would gather there, or at least the employees would share our excitement. Of course, the only people in the Roots store were foreign tourists, and the employees were American. Oh well . . .

While I felt like I had lost Canada, and that Canada might have lost Canada, I was very touched by the fact that I felt like Canada had not lost me. Canada has bestowed upon me many honours.

In 1993, I was made the honorary captain of the Team Canada under-21 team. I went to Calgary with Mackenzie, and during halftime, in front of a packed Saddledome (the Calgary Flames' home rink), I took penalty shots on Vladislav Tretiak, the famous Soviet goalie from the 1972 Summit Series. It was a dream come true. In fact, that experience prompted me to take power skating lessons, because there's nothing more humiliating than having nineteen thousand sophisticated Canadian hockey fans watch you ankle-skate. Still, it was a great honour, and Mackenzie and I got schnockered on Electric Avenue in Calgary. We met Lanny McDonald's cousin, or so he claimed.

In 2001, the Toronto Maple Leafs put a picture of me—from a promotional video they had invited me to

do—on one of their tickets. I got to keep a full set of gear and a complete uniform, including the socks.

In 2002, Toronto suffered an outbreak of SARS. Forty-four people died. Once the outbreak was contained, the Mayor of Toronto asked me if I would appear on *The Tonight Show* to let people know that Toronto was now safe. I went on and did my best. And for my efforts, a street in Toronto—in Scarborough, to be exact—was named after me. Mike Myers Drive. It's true: you can Google it.

Toronto also gave me a Key to the City. I was so blown away by this honour that I forgot to ask a few "key" questions like: Now that I have the Key to the City, is there a Lock to the City that I should know about? If that's the case, is there a Deadbolt to the City? Is there a Locksmith to the City in case I lose my Key to the City? Can I make copies of the Key to the City for my Buddies to the City? Is there a Churchkey to the City in case I need to open a Beer to the City? Is there a Key Fob to the City? If so, can the Key Fob to the City be customized to say, "This isn't a bald spot, it's a solar panel for a Sex Machine to the City"? That's all my Key to the City jokes.

In 2003, I got a star on Canada's Walk of Fame. On that trip, the Toronto Transit Commission gave me an official bus driver's uniform, including hat, tie, and tie pin. Cool. In 2004, I was voted number twenty in the CBC's *The Greatest Canadian* poll.

In 2013, the Canadian government issued a Mike Myers stamp. When I told my mum I was getting a stamp, the first thing she asked—in true, undercutting, Liverpool fashion—was, "Who else is getting a stamp?" followed by "What denomination is the stamp?" As if further inquiry was needed to determine where I fit on the "having a stamp" scale, ignoring the fact that having a stamp might be impressive enough on its own. My mother had temporarily lost sight of the great honour Canada was giving me.

In politics, Canada was losing sight of its traditions. On September 28, 2000, Pierre Trudeau died. I took his death very hard, and it underscored my fear that perhaps we had gotten even farther away from the promise of the Next Great Nation.

During my time out of country, Canada had a series of prime ministers who, to varying degrees, failed to carry the mantle of Trudeau's clarion call of defining Canadian uniqueness and exceptionalism. In many ways, these prime ministers were like the hapless magician who had to perform on *The Ed Sullivan Show* right after the Beatles had just played. Trudeau's first replacement, Joe Clark, a Progressive Conservative, was most notable for his nickname "Joe Who?" Political cartoonists had collectively agreed that any rendering of Joe Clark must include him wearing idiot-mittens. Clark lasted less than a year, only to see Trudeau return for his second and final tenure, during which I moved away from Canada.

But as I viewed Canada from England, and later from the United States, I watched my country turn away from Trudeau's level playing field–ism under a new prime minister, Brian Mulroney, the affable Irish-Canadian Progressive Conservative. He was "Canada's answer to" Ronald Reagan—which, of course, is absurd, as Ronald Reagan was so American that it would have been impossible for Canada to truly have an "answer" to him. Mulroney, like his antecedent Reagan, made strides to move away from a mixed economy, wherein the government benevolently referees the market to help working people, toward an unregulated, socially Darwinist, laissez-faire economy.

There were some positives while I was away. Canada gained its first female prime minister, Kim Campbell. Shortly after, Canada elected Jean Chrétien, who had worked with Trudeau. Chrétien tried to legalize gay marriage in Canada. By June 2005, legislation had been passed in eight of the ten provinces and the Yukon Territory. (Legislation passed under Chrétien's successor, Paul Martin, who a month later legalized same-sex marriage in Alberta, Prince Edward Island, Nunavut, and the Northwest Territories.) Chrétien also decided that Canada would not join the U.S.–led "coalition of the willing" and join the invasion of Iraq. We had

gone to Afghanistan, but Iraq felt like an unnecessary
war to him.

In 2006, Canada lost sight of its progressive traditions
when Stephen Harper, of the Conservative party, was
elected prime minister. If Mulroney loosened the jar of
reversing progressive policies, Harper opened the jar
wide, and then threw away the lid, and then smashed
the jar into a thousand pieces.

Also in 2006, Harper claimed, "You won't recognize
Canada when I'm done with it." Canada was no longer
going to be a place where experiments in progressivism
could take place for the benefit of the world. It was like
Trudeau had never happened. If Trudeau had turned up
the colour on the film of Canada to technicolor levels,
Harper made it black and white. Harper's tribalistic
policies valued purity, when Canada traditionally had
valued parity. We had turned into a junior America.
America Lite. Diet America. Only, without the dyna-
mism of the American Dream.

Harper played to racial stereotypes and fear.
He had his fans—he was in power for almost a full
decade. He was sensible to the extent that, in times
of an economic boom, he was fiscally conservative.
He was steady, he wasn't going to do anything crazy,
but if we had Harperism for three hundred years,
we would have had peace and order and the
cuckoo clock.

As a comedian whose work tends to be non-political,
I have struggled with taking a public stand on politics.
I have always felt that there's an unspoken deal with
my audience that I won't bait-and-switch them. I don't
invite the audience into my house on one premise, and
then, once they've taken off their shoes and are sitting

255

on my couch, make them read political pamphlets. So, I said nothing.

At least Canada was safe. I could turn to my American friends and say, "You see all that crazy shit that happens in the world? Well, it doesn't happen in Canada. I mean, sure, it can be a little boring at times, but it's safe."

But this was all to change.

By early 2014, I was a dual Canadian/American citizen living in New York City with an American wife, Kelly (I love you), two beautiful American

Corporal Nathan Cirillo.
A great Canadian.

children, and American friends. My brother Paul had become an American citizen living in Berkeley, California. I had sold my cottage north of Toronto, and although I did the occasional shout-out to Canada on talk shows, I really didn't hear anything about Canada, except the odd, sad story about the late Rob Ford. And while I'm happy the man is at peace, I never found his shenanigans and his tragic substance abuse at all funny. I'm not one for schadenfreude anyway.

On October 22, 2014, a lunatic from a theocratic death cult, who shall go unnamed, gunned down a Canadian soldier, Corporal Nathan Cirillo, while he stood guard in front of the National War Memorial in Ottawa.

Corporal Cirillo's gun contained no ammunition. Right-wingers have pointed to this as a flaw in Canadian progressivism, of course. They are missing two key points:

Top: Sergeant-at-Arms Kevin Vickers receives a standing ovation in the House of Commons.

Above: Here he is moments after protecting Parliament. Notice the object in his right hand. I never thought I would see the day. What a Canadian hero.

1. If Corporal Cirillo's weapon had been loaded, the murderer would now have had *two* weapons, and
2. There is tremendous symbolism in having a person guard a war memorial without the need for a loaded weapon.

The terrorist ran across the street, into the very heart of Canadian democracy, the Parliament Buildings, and a gun battle ensued.

That day, the sergeant-at-arms (the person responsible for protecting the Parliament) was a man named Kevin Vickers. At the sound of the first gunfire, he went to his office and retrieved his service weapon. He then engaged the terrorist. He did his job professionally, calmly, valiantly. It was over.

Later, it was revealed that there had been another attack two days earlier, in a parking lot outside a Veterans Affairs office in Saint-Jean-sur-Richelieu, Quebec. There, another Canadian hero, Warrant Officer Patrice Vincent, had been killed when a terrorist deliberately ran him and another soldier down with a

257

CANADA

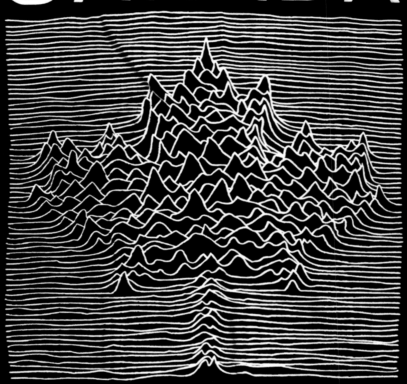

TRUE.NORTH.FREE

car. Of course, living in the States, I knew nothing of this until after the attack on Parliament Hill. I send my deepest condolences to the families of these heroes, and I send my sincerest gratitude for their service to Canada.

For me, and many Canadians, and certainly the families of the servicemen, this was a low point in the history of the country. During October of 2014, I did a lot of soul searching and, frankly, a lot of crying. Patrice Vincent seemed like a lovely man, and Nathan Cirillo had a son roughly my own son's age. And the thought that his son wouldn't be seeing his dad again, for me, transformed this tragic event from an emotional national news story to something deeply personal.

I was shocked, angry, and saddened, not only at the needless death of Corporal Cirillo and Warrant Officer Vincent, but saddened at the loss of the one bragging right about Canada that I had so heavily relied on, that this sort of thing didn't happen in Canada.

I believed we would never get a mission statement. We would never know not only who we are, but why we are, and we would slowly drift into a de facto consumerist suburb of the States.

It seemed like all hope was lost.

But wait . . .

CHAPTER SIX

A Canadian Future

Q UESTIONS BEGAN TO EMERGE.

How did this happen?

Are the Canadian security forces doing all that they can?

Are there more attacks coming?

What are we going to do?

Will we double down on security?

Will we start profiling people and rounding them up based on ethnicity or religion as opposed to strong intelligence?

Will we come up with a Canadian version of the Patriot Act?

Will Canadian fighter pilots send a disproportionate "message" by carpet bombing?

But there was a more important question. A fundamental question. It was the same fundamental question

261

that Canada has been asking itself over and over again since 1967:

Who are we going to be?

This question "Who are we going to be?" seemed to be a riddle that was all but unanswerable as I sat in America in the 1990s and 2000s, looking northward toward home. At that time, I thought, *Canada's not even trying to answer it anymore. They've given up.*

"Who are we going to be?" is a tough question for a country that doesn't even know who it is or why it is.

It's a question that seemed impossible to answer for a country born without a mission statement.

Would we ever get a mission statement?

Would this young, fragile nation that was created by default, an anomaly of "unwanted geography and inconsequential history," a country that evidently *is* depicted on a globe, but for all intents and purposes could be a "land sea," with grizzly bears being de facto sea monsters, a "never was," insecure country, ever answer the question "Why are we?"

Why are we? Seriously. Why bother?

As the scrum of international media surrounded Ottawa, the usual Canadian morbid platitudes crowded the airwaves, creating a sixty-cycle hum of banality.

But wait . . .

One Canadian voice rang out with the same clarity and gravitas of the carillon inside the Peace Tower of the Parliament Buildings. This Canadian voice spoke for the nation by saying:

ONE CANADIAN VOICE RANG OUT WITH THE SAME CLARITY AND GRAVITAS OF THE CARILLON INSIDE THE PEACE TOWER OF THE PARLIAMENT BUILDINGS.

262

In the days that follow, there will be questions, anger and perhaps confusion. This is natural, but we cannot let this get the better of us. Losing ourselves to fear and speculation is the intention of those who commit these heinous acts. They mean to shake us. We will remain resolved. They want us to forget ourselves. Instead, we will remember. We will remember who we are.

We are a proud democracy, a welcoming and peaceful nation, and a country of open arms and open hearts. We are a nation of fairness, of justice, and of the rule of law. We will not be intimidated into changing that. If anything, these are the values and principles to which we must hold on even tighter.

Our dedication to democracy and to the institutions we have built is the foundation of our society, and a continued belief in both will guide us correctly into the future. Staying true to our values in a time of crisis will make us an example to the world.

Criminals cannot and will not dictate to us how we act as a nation, how we govern ourselves, or how we treat each other. They cannot and will not dictate our values, and they do not get to decide how we use our shared public spaces.

Today, some speak of the loss of innocence in Canada. This is inaccurate. Canada is not and has never been innocent to the threats we face. And we know, as we have always known, that we are not immune. What is true is that we have never let those threats shape us, and we have never bowed to those who mean to undermine our values and our way of life. We have remained Canadians, and this is how we will carry on.

We will get answers to how and why this happened. They will be vital in preventing any future attack. And to our friends and fellow citizens in the Muslim community, Canadians know acts such as these committed in the name of Islam are an aberration of your faith. Continued mutual co-operation and respect will help prevent the influence of distorted ideological propaganda posing as religion.

We will walk forward together, not apart.

In the coming days, we will be inundated with pictures and videos showing what happened today. But there is one in particular we should all remember: the picture in our minds we have of Canadians helping and protecting Canadians. That is who we truly are, and it is who we shall continue to be.

The man who spoke those words was the leader of the Liberal Party, Justin Trudeau. He made the statement from Parliament Hill as he emerged from lockdown after the shooting.

Canada will be defined by its ideals alone. Fragile but very beautiful ideals like "I *am* my brother's keeper" and "No man is an island," and the notion that "the strength of a democracy is not how well we agree, but how well we disagree." Cooperation. Mutual respect. A level playing field. A culture that values *aligning with* fellow human beings as opposed to rewarding those that would *power over* them.

Canada is not a normal nation. And thank God. Let the other "normal" countries be defined by their cuisine, their banjos, their folklore, their entrenched oligarchic orthodoxies, or their handed-down superstitions. Fate and circumstance had conspired to evolve this underdog nation, Canada, into a beacon of progressive ideals for the world.

We weren't attacked by a hostile nation that day. We were attacked by a member of a repellent death cult, guided by a set of brutal, fascistic, misogynistic beliefs that are almost the inverse and opposite of our Canadian ideals. It's almost as if this backward, theocratic darkness allowed us to see our Canadian progressive principles in stark contrast. Sometimes the candle needs the dark.

Perhaps this terrible tragedy could mark the beginning of a movement toward a Canadian future. Justin Trudeau's father, Pierre Trudeau, had dedicated his life to such a culture, a Just Society. A Canadian future defined by us, for us. A country that could become the panglossic peaceable kingdom that Pierre Trudeau had imagined.

Canada didn't double down on right-wing security measures. We returned to peace, order, and good

government. And in the words of the great English poet Nick Lowe, as sung by another great English poet, Elvis Costello, "What's so funny about peace, love, and understanding?"

Soon after the Parliament Hill shootings of 2014, I went up to Toronto to visit my mum and my brother Peter and his beautiful family. It had been a while since I had been to see the Leafs play, and although they lost, there really is nothing like "the good old hockey game."

Hockey Night in Canada asked me to say a few words about the events in Ottawa. I wasn't sure I had anything to say, to be honest. It hadn't been my style to wax political in interviews, but the Parliament Hill shootings were different. It was very emotional for me. I concurred with Justin Trudeau that Canada should not change in the face of this tragedy. Yet, I'm a human being, and my country had been attacked.

I WANTED TO MAKE THE POINT THAT NO ONE SHOULD EVER CONFUSE CANADA'S CIVILITY FOR WEAKNESS.

I was angry. I wanted to make the point that no one should ever confuse Canada's civility for weakness. Any adversary would do so at their own peril. I'm reminded of Passchendaele, Dieppe, Juno, the Scheldt Estuary, Korea, and Afghanistan, just to name a few. We are a peace-loving nation, but when we've been forced to fight we have historically done so heroically, knowing that we fight for a collection of beautiful ideals. Canadian ideals.

The shootings at Parliament Hill changed me.

Articles detailing the reactions of various Canadian political figures showed a disturbing, and growing, "normalization" of Islamaphobia. This struck me as the antithesis of the Canadian ethos.

———

For months prior to the October 19, 2015 election, I was asked repeatedly, by both Canadian and American news outlets, to comment on the election. I declined each time. But the election race was close, time was running out, and I felt that Canadian ideals were at stake, and that this election would be a defining moment for Canada.

As fate would have it, my good friend and fellow Liverpool FC fanatic, John Oliver, was dedicating an episode of his show, HBO's *Last Week Tonight*, to the Canadian election. John Oliver had been following Stephen Harper's growing xenophobia. This episode of his show would air the day before the election. He called and asked me if I would join him in imploring the Canadian electorate not to vote for Stephen Harper.

I agreed.

The first line of John Oliver's piece about the Canadian election went as follows: "Canada, the country you think

about so little . . . That's it. End of sentence." However, Oliver, in his brilliance, went on to describe, with rapier wit, the state of Canadian politics. Even I didn't know the full extent to which Canada had reversed its progressive policies. As I said, I live in the States. And you never hear any news about Canada when you live in the States.

At all.

Ever.

And so, at 11:30 p.m. on October 18, literally on the eve of the election, I put on a Mountie suit, got on a snow plow, and John and I urged Canada not to vote for Harper.

It made the news in Canada and the United States that I had taken such a definitive stand. I don't know if it made a difference, but either way, I was happy the next day, when Justin Trudeau, leader of the Liberal Party and son of my hero, Pierre Elliot Trudeau, was elected.

> I RECOGNIZED IN THESE APPROVAL-SEEKING PRIME MINISTERS THE YOUNGER BROTHER WHO WANTED TO TAG ALONG WITH THE COOLER OLDER BROTHER.

On November 4, 2015, Justin Trudeau was sworn into office as Canada's twenty-third prime minister. One of the first things that happened for Prime Minister Justin Trudeau was a phone call from President Barack Obama of the United States of America. There were the usual pleasantries and congratulations, but supposedly, Prime Minister Trudeau declared on that first call that Canada would not take part in the fighting in Syria and Iraq and that he was recalling the Canadian fighter jets that were participating in the air war against ISIS. Audaciously, Trudeau did not want to put Canadian

servicemen in harm's way without either a game plan or an exit strategy. There had been a long list of Canadian prime ministers who had sought the approval of American presidents. Being the youngest of three, I recognized in these approval-seeking prime ministers the younger brother who wanted to tag along with the cooler older brother. "Where ya guys goin', eh? Mum said I could hang out with you guys." Prime Minister Justin Trudeau, it seems, was going to buck that trend.

Moreover, shortly after his call with President Obama, Prime Minister Trudeau welcomed twenty-five thousand Syrian refugees to Canada, welcoming them literally with open arms. A Canadian children's choir sang the Syrian anthem on their arrival. I was moved to tears. It was the inverse and opposite of Islamaphobia.

Trudeau had pledged in his campaign that he would run a budget deficit for his first three years in office, to ease the effects of the recent austerity measures that were almost exclusively hurting working people. In America, running on a platform of a budget deficit would be deemed political suicide, akin to outlawing beer at NASCAR races. In a bold move that would have shocked even his father, Trudeau the younger formed a cabinet that was 50 percent female. Some found this move to be either cosmetic, arbitrary, or foolhardy. A reporter asked him, "Why do women make up 50 percent of your cabinet?"

Trudeau replied, "Because it's 2015."

"Welcome home," said the PM as he greeted newly arrived Syrian refugees.

Just watch him.

What the fuddle-duddle.

On a personal note, Trudeau recently put forth a bill that would legalize assisted suicide for the terminally ill. Well before my father got Alzheimer's, he made me promise him that I would pull the plug should he ever get a terminal diagnosis involving either prolonged pain or a vegetative state. And in the hellish, torturous, cruel last year of his Alzheimer's ravaged "life," if the doctors had given me a button to press that would end his suffering, I would have hit that button faster and harder than any overcaffeinated aunt who thinks she has the answer on *Family Feud*. (See? I'm morbid too.)

God bless Justin Trudeau. Talk about perfect legislation for an imperfect world. Equally bold and pragmatic is Trudeau's pending legislation to legalize marijuana.

While the big government culture-identity program that I've called the Next Great Nation movement of 1967–1976 was abandoned, it doesn't mean that it failed completely. One can argue that it created Justin Trudeau. One can look to Hollywood, the world of architecture, and music, and see the fruits of that investment. In many ways, it's like America's space program. While that big government program is now virtually abandoned, even the most cynical amongst us couldn't call NASA a failure. They put a man on the moon, for God's sake. I'm heartened to see that Prime Minister Justin Trudeau has promised to increase funding for the CBC.

If we are to believe, like I do, that Canada now finally has a mission statement and the necessary leadership, perhaps

271

Canada is now poised to be the country most likely to succeed in a rapidly changing world. Canada is ready.

Canada already has infrastructure, natural resources, the most fresh water of any country, one of the largest fishing banks in the world, nearly limitless amounts of timber, vast oil reserves, hydroelectric power, nuclear power, diamonds, and other precious metals up the wazoo.

Geographically, we are next to the economic powerhouse that is America, the markets of Asia, and the emerging economy of Russia. Because of our NATO ties, we have a strong connection to Europe.

Climate change may, sadly, devastate much of the world. However, because of our northern geography, Canada may temporarily benefit from global warming. It may give us a second growing season, which is the usual precursor for cultures that have distinctive cuisines (see: Italy). Also, if we're smart, we will invest in clean technology. Maybe the fact that we never produced a Canadian car will now be a blessing, because perhaps we can make the best electric car. And Canada could do this. The country is very stable, it values civility, it has a harmonious and diverse population, no internal strife, one of the lowest crime rates in the world, one of the highest literacy rates in the world, and is often voted one of the top three places in the world to live. Recently, Canada was ranked by millennials as the number 1 place

in the world to live. We also have universal healthcare, which may be Canada's greatest gift to the world.

Of course, we argue about universal healthcare in Canada, and the system is not perfect. But the arguments about healthcare are usually about how best to improve the system, not whether there should be a system. Healthcare is not easy, people. And I'm going to make a big, bold statement: I think a healthcare safety net is exactly what all governments should be providing.

In early March 2016, I got a call that I had been invited to the White House for a state dinner honouring Canada's new prime minister, Justin Trudeau. This was mind-blowing to me. I was so excited and so honoured. It was the first White House state dinner for a Canadian prime minister in twenty years.

State dinners at the White House are full of pomp and circumstance. They're very formal affairs—the dress is black tie, and strict etiquette is observed. I was afraid I wasn't going to know anybody, but thankfully Lorne Michaels was there, as were my friends Michael J. Fox and Ryan Reynolds and his lovely wife, Blake Lively.

273

Tradition has it that, as you enter the White House, you proceed to the receiving line to meet the president and the guest head of state. I was so nervous to meet Justin Trudeau that I was strangely comfortable having a conversation about foreign policy with the person in the line ahead of me, House Minority Leader Nancy Pelosi. She is very nice.

It was just about to be my turn to meet President Obama, Mrs. Obama, Prime Minister Trudeau, and Mrs. Grégoire-Trudeau. I could tell that Obama really liked Trudeau, and that made me happy. I was heartened to see how incredibly handsome all four of them were.

I know it's shallow, but isn't it awesome that our prime minister and his wife are hotties?

I shook President Obama's hand and moved down the line to Prime Minister Trudeau.

Protocol dictates a handshake. However, the Prime Minister gave me a hug and jokingly said, "Mike, thank you so much. You know that thing you did on John Oliver? It got me elected." I laughed and thought, *That's a great joke.* Of course, it's unlikely that two minutes on HBO would change an election. Then I thought, *What got him elected was his eloquent speech after the Parliament Hill shootings.* Then I thought, *Wait, he hugged me!*

My wife, Kelly, and I took our seats and listened to two of the greatest speeches I've ever heard in my life, delivered by two of the greatest orators I've ever seen live. The speeches were heartfelt and funny. There was genuine love in the room, both between Prime Minister Trudeau and President Obama and, if I daresay, between Canada and the United States. We really are brothers. It struck me how remarkable it is that we have the longest undefended border in the world. I felt grateful to have grown up in a country that had peace, order, and good government. A country that enabled a child of working-class immigrants to one day attend a state dinner at the White House, honouring his prime minister. I was very proud of Canada that night.

I love Canada. Canada is home. When I see Canadians on the street, anywhere in the world, I get very happy. I love that the entire interaction often involves people simply saying hello and then telling me the town in Canada that they're from. I'll be on the street and a fellow Canadian will say, "Mike . . . Kamloops!" And that's it. Nothing else has to be said. I love that!

I'm so confident in Canada's future. We know ourselves now. I can't wait for my kids, who are American, to be old enough to be proud that their old man comes from that cool country to the north that has tried harder than any other country in the history of the world to get it right. I know they're going to be proud to be American. What great gifts has America given the world? Great music, movies . . . they put a man on the moon.

Canada may not have put a man on the moon, but it's been awfully nice to the man on earth. And perhaps that will be Canada's greatest legacy.

But having said that, wouldn't it be nice if Canada *did* put a man on the moon? We can do both. Now.

Canada, I have known you for fifty-three years. Without you, I'd be nothing.

Happy 150th birthday.

I love you, Canada.

And I always will.

ACKNOWLEDGEMENTS

I want to thank Kristin Cochrane at Penguin Random House Canada for asking me to write this book.

I want to thank my editor, Tim Rostron.

I want to thank Amy Black, Susan Burns, Erin Cooper, Valerie Gow, Ward Hawkes, Carla Kean, Terri Nimmo, Scott Sellers, Melanie Tutino, and everyone at Penguin Random House Canada who had a hand in this project.

I want to acknowledge Northrop Frye C.C., Malcolm Gladwell C.M., Marshall McLuhan C.C., and Margaret Atwood C.C. for their genius.

I want to acknowledge Andrew H. Malcolm for his fantastic book *The Canadians*.

I want to acknowledge Douglas Coupland O.C., O.B.C. for being a great Canadian and for his fabulous Souvenir of Canada books.

I want to thank Mel Berger.

I want to thank Jerry Levitan for his tireless support.

I want to thank Major-General Sir Isaac Brock for defending Canada at the Battle of Queenston Heights during the War of 1812.

I want to thank hockey.

I want to thank Glenn Cochrane, CFTO-TV News, for reminding us that wherever we go, we're never too far from a coupla lovely ladies.

I want to thank Paul Henderson C.M. for "The Goal." And I want to thank Phil Esposito O.C. for "The Speech."

I want to thank Canada. Well done.

I want to thank Corporal Nathan Cirillo and Warrant Officer Patrice Vincent, as well as the rest of the Canadian Armed Forces, for their service and their sacrifice.

I want to thank Mr. Gross and Mr. Maclean, my Television course teachers at Stephen Leacock Collegiate Institute, for believing.

I want to thank Andrew Alexander and Sally Cochrane for hiring me at Second City.

I want to thank Christopher Ward for his friendship and guidance.

I want to thank Canada House in London.

I want to thank Pierre Elliott Trudeau for believing that Canada would be the Next Great Nation and for making Justin Trudeau.

I want to thank Justin Trudeau for carrying the torch.

I want to thank Dan Aykroyd C.M. for his genius and his generosity.

I want to thank Lorne Michaels C.M. for being the Canadian Godfather.

I want to thank Barry Cohen for the cover photo and his friendship.

I want to thank Andrew Hollingworth and Mackenzie Cyr for their expert assistance.

I want to thank Gavin de Becker for his insight and for being the funniest civilian in the world.

I want to thank Rob Cohen for being as Canadian as possible under the circumstances.

I want to thank my fantastic manager, Jason Weinberg, for having my back.

I want to thank David Mackenzie for being my best friend and for lending me some of his hilarious observations about Canada.

I want to thank my brother Peter Myers for being so smart, so funny, and so Canadian.

I want to thank my brother Paul Myers for also being smart and funny, and for his contributions to this book.

I want to thank my parents, Eric and Bunny Myers.

I want to thank my children, Spike, Sunday, and Paulina, for becoming future Canadians.

Above all, I would like to thank my wife, Kelly. I love you, Kelly.

vi. Portrait of Queen Elizabeth II by Mike Myers.

viii–ix. Hollywood Walk of Fame.

x. John Candy in: PLANES , TRAINS AND AUTOMOBILES © Paramount Pictures. All Rights Reserved.

1. Centennial Leaf: Stuart Ash, 1966/Government of Canada; Polaroid frame: FINDEEP/ Shutterstock.com.

2. Mike Myers and Ryan Gosling on *SNL*: © Dana Edelson/NBCU Photo Bank via Getty Images.

4. (top left) Drake with Mounties: George Pimentel/WireImage/Getty Images; (top right) *Views*: Young Money Entertainment/Cash Money Records; Marshal McLuhan: CBC Still Photo Collection/Robert Ragsdale.

7. Centennial Train: Library and Archives Canada, Acc. No. 1984-4-1508. © Government of Canada.

8. The Canada 150 logo: Ariana Cuvin, 2015/Courtesy of The Department of Canadian Heritage/© Government of Canada.

10. B.C. totem poles: *Chief Wakas Kwakiutl pole*, Doug Cranmer, 1987, based on pole from the 1890s; *Thunderbird House Post Totem Pole*, Charlie James, early 1900s; *Sky Chief Totem Pole*, Tim Paul and Art Thompson, 1988/photo by Paul Myers.

11. Polaroid frame: FINDEEP/Shutterstock.com.

13. *Captain Canuck* issue 1: Captain Canuck ® & © Copyright Richard Comely 1975–2016. Permission granted through Chapterhouse Publishing.

15. (top) TTC streetcar and Ricky Receptacle: Paul Myers; (bottom) Ricky Receptacle: Courtesy of Steven Petric.

16. *Canadian Mounties vs. Atomic Invaders*: Courtesy of The Everett Collection.

17. Mary Pickford bust and plaque: Kate Panek.

18. The Myers family's backyard, Scarborough: Mike Myers; Polaroid frame: FINDEEP/Shutterstock.com.

19. The Beaverlodge Beaver: Ron Erwin/AllCanadaPhotos.com.

20. Major-General Sir Isaac Brock: George Theodore Berthon, c. 1883. Government of Ontario Art Collection/Archives of Ontario.

21. "Canada's 'enthusiasm' for census brings down StatsCan website": Peter Bowman/CBC/Twitter.

22–23. Avro Arrow CF-105 model: Hobbycraft Canada; Courtesy of Scott Nimmo. Photo by Kate Panek.

24. (top) Wayne and Shuster: CBC Still Photo Collection; (middle) © Doug Henning: NBCU Photo Bank via Getty; (bottom) Beatles: © Parlophone/EMI.

25. OPP patch: Ontario Provincial Police.

26. Margaret Atwood: © Liam Sharp 2016.

28. (background) John McCrae's "In Flanders Fields": Archive.org; folded paper: © Sharpshot/Dreamstime.com; poppy: © Andras Csontos/Dreamstime.com.

30. SickKids: Kate Panek.

31. *Les Troubbes de Johnny*: Jacques Godbout/NFB; *Bang Bang Baby*: Scythia Films, JoBro Film Finances & Productions, Revolver Films; airplane screens: Dutourdumonde Photography/Shutterstock.com and Air Canada/photo by Paul Myers.

33. *The Sweet Hereafter*: © Ego Film Arts.

32. *Scanners*: Courtesy of Laurem Productions Inc.

34. Map: dalmingo/Shutterstock.com.

38. (top) Toy soldier: Courtesy of Jennifer Lum; (bottom) box of Girl Guide Cookies: Girl Guides of Canada.

39. Toy soldier: Courtesy of Jennifer Lum.

40. Paul Anka: Popperfoto/Getty Images.

41. *Canada Firsts*, Ralph Nader: Courtesy of McClelland & Stewart.

45. Polaroid frame: FINDEEP/Shutterstock.com.

47. Queen Elizabeth II: Chronicle/Alamy Stock Photo.

48. Toronto Maple Leafs patch: Maple Leafs Sports and Entertainment.

50. Château Frontenac: Harvey Meston/Archive Photos/Getty Images.

53. Polaroid frame: FINDEEP/Shutterstock.com.

56. Honest Ed's: Kate Panek.

57. Eaton's catalogue: Eaton's/Sears Canada Inc.

60. Saturn V lifting off: Courtesy of the NASA History Office and Kennedy Space Center.

61. Bob and Doug McKenzie: © MGM/Entertainment Pictures/ZUMA Press Inc./Alamy Stock Photo.

62. Irv Weinstein: ABC/WKBW-TV; TV set: ghenadie/Shutterstock.com.

65. Joni Mitchell: Jack Robinson/Hulton Archive/Getty Images.

68. Stompin' Tom Connors: CBC Still Photo Collection/Paul Smith.

69. Canadian Tire logo: Canadian Tire Corporation Ltd.

71. Glenn Cochrane: Jim Wilkes/Toronto Star via Getty Images.

72. CFTO-TV pin: CTV/Bell Media.

74. Canada Wordmark on a freight train: Paul Myers.

77. 1050 CHUM pamphlet: CHUM Ltd./Bell Media.

80. *Shrek*: Chris Polk/FilmMagic/Getty Images.

83. (top left) *The Hilarious House of Frightenstein*: CHCH-DT/Channel Zero; (top right) *The Friendly Giant*: CBC Still Photo Collection; Polaroid frame: FINDEEP/Shutterstock.com.

84. (top) *The King of Kensington*: CBC Still Photo Collection/Harold Whyte; (bottom) North York apartments: Ward Hawkes.

85. Clairton stereo record player: Clairtone Sound Corporation Ltd.

87. (top) Canadian Tire money: Canadian Tire Corporation Ltd.

88. TTC logo: © Toronto Transit Commission/photo by Paul Myers; Mike Myers' TTC Metropass and TTC Student Cards from Sir John A. Macdonald Collegiate and Stephen Leacock Collegiate.

91. Milk bag in jug: Kate Panek.

92. Lonesome Charlie ad: Jordan Wines/Constellation Brands.

93. (left) Tahiti Treat: PepsiCo Canada; (right) Hostess Hickory Sticks: Dr Pepper Snapple Group.

94. Volkswagen Beetle next to Toronto City Hall: City of Toronto Archives, Fonds 124, File 2, Item 3.

97. (top) Vintage *Hockey Night in Canada* logo: CBC Still Photo Collection; (bottom) Ball and Hockey Playing Prohibited: Paul Myers; Polaroid frame: FINDEEP/Shutterstock.com.

98. Hockey cards: Topps® Hockey Trading Card used courtesy of The Topps Company Inc.

99. CNE at dusk: Courtesy of © John Hinde Archive www.johnhindearchive.com.

100. CNE: City of Toronto Archives, Fond 1526, File 94, Item 22.

102. Labelle: Gijsbert Hanekroot/Redferns Collection/Getty Images.

105. Wrigley's Spearmint Chewing Gum: Wrigley Canada.

108. *Range Ryder and the Calgary Kid*: CBC Still Photo Collection/Norman Chamberlin.

119. Beatles monument, Liverpool: © age fotostock/Alamy Stock Photo.

111. *Motion Picture #1*: Paul Myers.

116. Portrait of Pierre Elliot Trudeau: Mike Myers.

117: Polaroid Frame: FINDEEP/Shutterstock.com.

120. CBC logo, 1974-1986: CBC Still Photo Collection.

122. Expo 67 poster: *The 1967 World Exhibition - Show of the Century* © Government of Canada. Reproduced with the permission of Library and Archives Canada (2016). Source: Library and Archives Canada/Canadian Corporation for the 1967 World Exhibition fonds/e000988792.

124. Trudeau victory: Reg Innell/Toronto Star via Getty Images.

126. (top) Sam Sniderman: Toronto Star Archives/Toronto Star via Getty Images; (bottom) Sam the Record Man, Toronto: Toronto Star Archives/Toronto Star via Getty Images.

127. 7Up Rock Caps poster and cap: PepsiCo Canada.

128. (top) Esso Power Player album: Esso/Imperial Oil Ltd./NHL; (bottom) Neil Young: Frazer Harrison/Getty Image.

129. (top) Shell Canada Commemorative Medallions: Shell Canada Ltd.; (bottom) Esso Power Player album cover: Esso/Imperial Oil Ltd./NHL.

130. Cherry Blossom Candy: Hershey Canada Inc.

131. Hostess ketchup chips: Joad Henry/cc via Flickr; Dr Pepper Snapple Group.

132. John and Yoko "War Is Over" campaign: Frank Barratt/Hulton Archive/Getty Images.

133. Ritchie Yorke: Ron Bull/Toronto Star via Getty Images.

134. *Ultimatum: Oil or War?*, Richard Rohmer: Simon & Schuster.

135. Pierre Trudeau with John and Yoko: THE CANADIAN PRESS/Peter Bregg.

136. ParticipACTION badge: ParticipACTION Canada.

139. Pierre Laporte discovered: Montreal La Presse via THE CANADIAN PRESS.

140. Downtown Toronto, 1970s: Robert Taylor/cc via Flickr.

143. McGuinness Vodka ad: Chris Yaneff Ltd./Corby Spirit and Wine Ltd.

144. Phil Esposito: Photo by Frank Lennon/Toronto Star via Getty Images.

146. Paul Henderson's iconic goal: Frank Lennon/Toronto Star.

147. (right) CN Tower nears completion: Robert Taylor/cc via Flickr; Polaroid frame: FINDEEP/
Shutterstock.com.

151. Gilda Radner: © NBCU Photo Bank via Getty Images.

152. *The Hart and Lorne Terrific Hour*: CBC Still Photo Collection.

155. (top) Polaroid frame: FINDEEP/Shutterstock.com; (bottom) Eaton's lucky shoe: Mike Deal,
Winnipeg Free Press. Reproduced with permission.

156. "The Van" superimposed beneath a Canada wordmarked train: Paul Myers.

159. Polaroid frame: FINDEEP/Shutterstock.com.

162. Regina: © Dmitry Kaminsky/Alamy Stock Photo.

163. Polaroid frame: FINDEEP/Shutterstock.com.

165. Witches swearing allegiance to the devil: Philip and Elizabeth De Bay/© Stapleton Collection/
Corbis Historical/Corbis via Getty Images.

167. *Never Cry Wolf*, Farley Mowat: Dell Publishing/courtesy of Penguin Random House LLC.

168. Pentagram: Stanislas de Guaita, 1897.

169. Vancouver: Paul Myers; Polaroid frame: FINDEEP/Shutterstock.com.

170: Toronto, 1984: Paul Myers.

171. Peter Cook and Dudley Moore as Clive and Derek: Michael Putland/Hulton Archive/Getty Images.

173. Notting Hill Gate, 1983: TedQuackenbush/cc via Flickr.

174. The Cameron House, Toronto: Paul Myers.

175. Morwenna Banks: © Ray Burmiston.

178. Mullarkey and Myers, Primrose Hill, London: Courtesy of Charles Martin.

183. Polaroid frame: FINDEEP/Shutterstock.com.

186. *John and Yoko: A Love Story*: Carson Productions/CBS.

196. Del Close: The Post-Rational Players/The Second City.

187. Polaroid frame: FINDEEP/Shutterstock.com.

198. Bomb: DVARG/Shutterstock.com.

201. Dave Foley: Courtesy of Byron J. Bignell.

203. Mark Myers is totally awesome, not at all bogus: uncredited newspaper clipping.

204. (top) Mike Myers and Lorne Michaels: Steve Higgins; (bottom) Louis Malle: Jean-Pierre
Bonnotte/Gamma-Rapho via Getty Images.

205. *Lacombe, Lucien* poster: AF archive/Alamy Stock Photo.

210. Aurora, Ontario, postcard: Smallwares Distributors Co., Toronto.

211. Let's Go Canada! wartime poster: Henri Eveleigh/Government of Canada.

215. "You are the Wayne to my Garth": USA Today/Twitter.

216. Leslie Nielsen: © NBCU Photo Bank via Getty Images.

217. Conan O'Brien: The LIFE Picture Collection/Getty Images.

219. Don Pardo: © Fred Hermansky/NBCU Photo Bank via Getty Images.

221. Phil Hartman and Mike Myers: Barry King/Hulton Archive/Getty Images.

222. Mike Myers and Phil Hartman on *SNL*: © Al Levin/NBCU Photo Bank via Getty Images.

230. Dr. Brian May tweet: Brian May/Twitter.

231. (top) Lotta Hitschmanova: Harvard Square Library; (middle) Rosa Klebb: United Artists Corporation/Danjaq LLC; (bottom) Frau Farbissina: New Line Cinema/Warner Bros.

235. Polaroid frame: FINDEEP/Shutterstock.com.

239. "Simon" on *SNL*: © Alan Singer/NBCU Photo Bank via Getty Images.

240. Kraft Dinner: Kraft Canada Inc.

242. TTC logo on subway train: © Toronto Transit Commission/photo by Paul Myers.

243. Maple Leaf Gardens: Paul Myers.

244. (top) Tallest buildings in the world: Rama/Wikimedia Commons; (bottom) Blackberry phone: Fairfax Media via Getty Images.

245. "'Who' Tall Are You?" mirror in The Canadian Brewhouse: Rob Cohen.

246. Early Nunavut license plate: THE CANADIAN PRESS/Nathan Denette.

247. Polaroid frame: FINDEEP/Shutterstock.com.

250. (middle) Mike Myers star on Canada's Walk of Fame: Kate Panek.

251. Mike Myers stamp: © Canada Post, 2014.

252. (top) Joe Clark: Ron Bull/Toronto Star via Getty Images; (bottom) Reagan and Mulroney: Erin Combs/Toronto Star via Getty Images.

253. Pierre Trudeau: Tim Graham/Hulton Archive/Getty Images.

254. Mural at Queen St. West and Dovercourt: Kate Panek.

256. Corporal Nathan Cirillo: © All rights reserved. Photograph of Cpl Cirillo reproduced with the permission of DND/CAF, 2016.

257. (top) Sergeant-at-Arms Kevin Vickers receives standing ovation: THE CANADIAN PRESS/Adrian Wyld; (bottom) Sergeant-at-Arms Kevin Vickers after the attack: Mike Depaul/CBC News.

260. Justin Trudeau being sworn in as Prime Minister: THE CANADIAN PRESS/Sean Kilpatrick.

261. Pierre and Justin Trudeau: Journal de Montreal/QMI; Polaroid frame: FINDEEP/Shutterstock.com.

265. Justin Trudeau wins the election: Winnipeg Free Press. Reproduced with permission.

267. Mike Myers on *Last Week Tonight with John Oliver*: HBO.

269. Justin Trudeau interviewed by American press: CNN.

270. Justin Trudeau greets newly arrived Syrian family: THE CANADIAN PRESS/Nathan Denette.

272. Pierre Trudeau in the NWT: THE CANADIAN PRESS/Peter Bregg.

273. Justin Trudeau in a meeting: Justin Trudeau/Twitter.

Note to readers: Page numbers in italics refer to illustrations (or captions) that appear on pages that are separate from the main discussion. To avoid duplication, illustrations on the same page (or within the same range of pages) as a subject have not been listed.

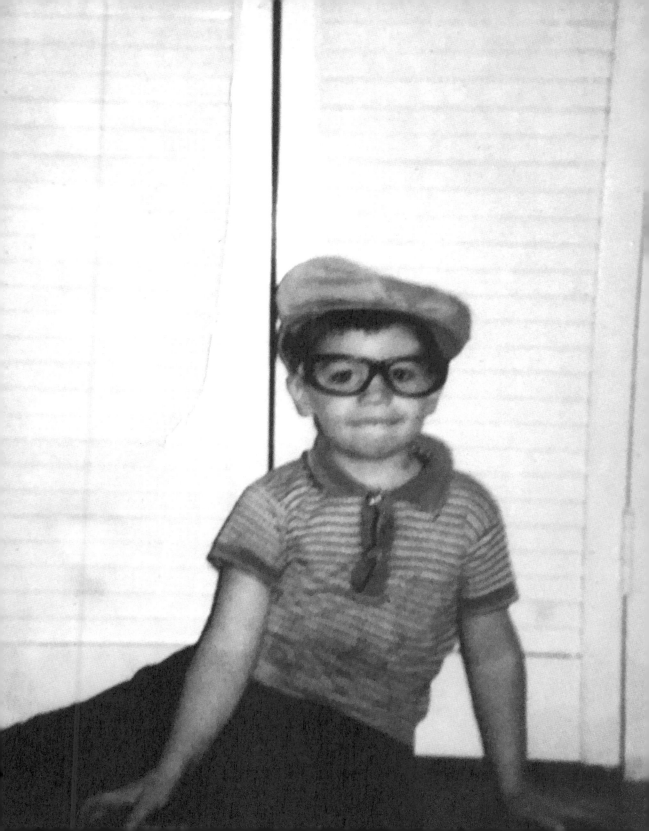

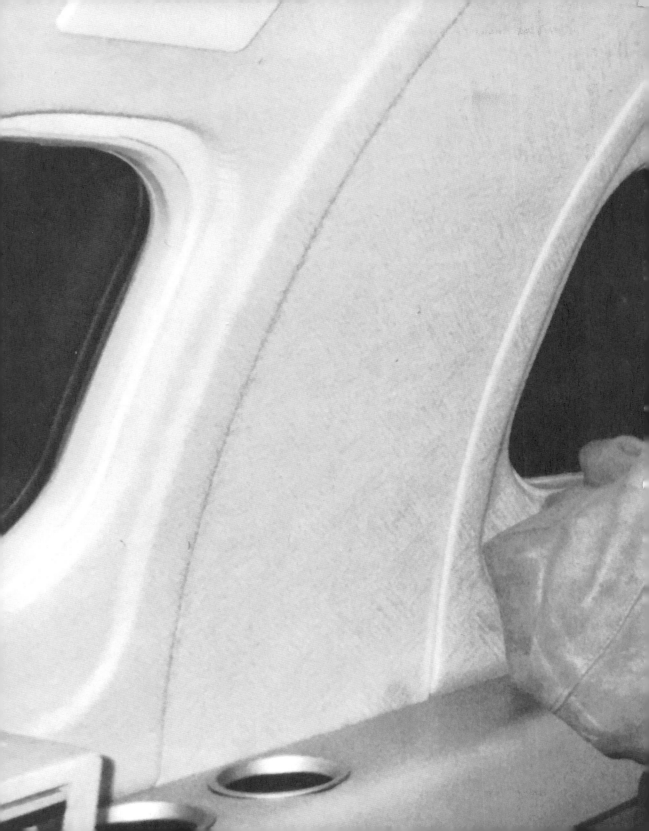